Introduction

We moved to the lovely Costa Blanca North around eight years ago, and I can honestly say that we have had no regrets at all in leaving grey, cold, crowded England. Life here is as good as it gets; the weather is kind, the people lovely, the food and drink excellent, the whole lifestyle an object lesson in how life should be lived. Sounds wonderful? Take my word for it, it is!

Before we moved, I thought I had done as much research as it was possible to do. I thought I had all the answers at my fingertips; and bear in mind I used to work for the British Library, so if I couldn´t be confident that I had done my research well and thoroughly, who could? I read numerous "how to" guides, haunted the internet, made sure I kept up with all the Costa Blanca local papers on line. It was only after we had made the move, alas, that I realised that I had neglected the one, vital thing that **all** expats don´t understand, and it´s a real Catch-22 situation. You see, until you move, until you get over here and start settling in, you suddenly realise that whilst all that research is lovely, you still don´t have the key to **living** here.

Why? Simply because *you don't know what the right questions are to ask!* You really do have to live here to know how true this simple fact is. The manuals and the internet articles are a help, of course, but they are far less than half the story. For instance, you may have read that you have to contact DWP (formerly DHSS) at Newcastle to get a letter stating you are not eligible for healthcare in the UK anymore, and that this letter will allow you to get state healthcare in Valencia. It certainly will, but **only** if you are in receipt of a state pension and even if you are a UK state pensioner, how, exactly, do you get that letter in the right hands to access the system? Your estate agent has made sure your new house in the Costa Blanca has electricity connected, so why has it suddenly gone off? And why on earth has your meter actually disappeared?? And how do you get it back??? (For the answers, read on!). You're sure I have to pay income tax in Spain? How on earth do I do that? And why do I have to make an annual tax declaration when I don't earn enough to pay income tax? What do you mean; you pay car tax in Spain? None of the cars have a tax disc, do they? And cars have to have MOT's? You're joking!

These – and a thousand other questions, and of course more importantly the answers to those questions – are the things I wished I had known about before we packed our bags and left the UK to live in sunnier climes.

Because, I am afraid, in laid-back Spain, if you don't ask the correct question, you will either not get an answer at all (other than a shrug of the shoulders) or a good-natured stab at an answer that is likely to cause more confusion than anything else. At the very best, you will get an answer to the question you asked, but nothing else.

You will not be told that this is just part of a process, and there are lots more you need to do. Nothing will be volunteered, and if you don't know what the right question is, you will find yourself sinking rapidly. Unfortunately, bureaucracy in Spain is immense and unbending. Rules and regulations change regularly, and it can be a nightmare if you don't understand the basics. Once you understand the processes, it becomes second nature, and you stop worrying. It took me years to get to this stage!

The good news is that it's not just aimed at us expats. Spaniards are equally annoyed by it but they, of course, have the distinct advantages of both speaking the language, and being brought up to expect problem. We frequently used to see the owner of our local garden centre at the Ayuntamiento (Town Hall). We would exchange greetings, and then raise a questioning eyebrow. The response from Carlos was always the same; he would clutch his hair, raise his eyes to heaven and then shake his head before making for the nearest bar. A brandy or two seemed to help matters, because next time we were there, so was he!

If at first you don't succeed....

The purpose of this manual is, then, to tell you what questions you should be asking – now! Before you move! And, of course, to give you either an answer, or to tell you where you can find that answer. I am probably better qualified than many to know what those questions are, and to provide either answers to them, or at the very least point you in the right direction to find those all important answers. (Says she, modestly!).

Not only have I lived here for eight years, but for 3 of those years I was Secretary of our local Vecinos ("Neighbours") organization, and I coped daily with questions like, "Help! Iberdrola have cut off my electricity, and I'm in England!" Or, "Help, I bought a bargain villa here and now the local council says I owe them €4,000 for something called "a plus valia"! Or, "Help, I've been burgled – who do I ring?" The answer, generally, was naturally "I'll do it for you", and I have to admit that during the course of those 3 years I learned an awful lot about Spanish bureaucracy, and – more importantly – how to get things done. Even better – I learned an awful lot about how to stop things happening in the first place.

To give you an example of "how it works" at the Council. We recently bought a new car. In Spain, this invariably involves a fat pile of documentation which must be handed over to your dealer in good time. Not just paperwork for your old car, which you are part-exchanging, but lots of identification documentation for you. We were asked to produce our passports, our NIE numbers, our Residencias, and our Padrons. (Don't worry, all these documents, and how to get them, are explained later).

Everything except the Padron was to hand, but we had to get a new copy of that from the Ayuntamiento; and when you read the tale of woe that follows, please bear in mind that I had been having meetings with the Mayor in the Ayuntamiento every 3 months for a couple of years, and knew many of the staff by name. We went down to see Vicente, in the "Extranjeros" (Foreigners) Office. Handed over our NIE numbers, passports, old Padron and Residencia certificates. He glanced through the pile, prodded our Residencias, and said "No." Why not? We enquired. It was, he said, out of date. We pointed out that the new style certificates didn´t have an expiry date. No matter, he said. It had been issued over 5 years before, and hence was terminated. We checked with our accountants, who confirmed that the Residencias were fine, and had not expired. Back to Vicente, who listened politely and then pointed at his computer; the computer, apparently, said the Residencias had expired, so as far as he was concerned, they had expired. We must, he said, go to the Guardia Civil offices and get a new Residencia. Back to our accountants, who said again that they had not expired. They very kindly offered to speak to Vicente, and telephoned him for us. Great, we thought, problem solved. Vicente smiled at us when we went in the next day, and said …. No. We went to the Guardia. Nonsense, they said. The new style

—
7

certificates did not expire, so hence they could not issue us with a new one. By this time, our lovely new car was ready for collection, and we were at our wits´ end. We couldn´t get a new Padron because Vicente insisted our Residencias had expired, but we couldn´t get a new Residencia, because the Guardia said we didn´t need one. No Padron, no car.

Finally, I persuaded a very irate Vicente to ring the Guardia offices, and speak to the very nice young man we had seen the day before. A few moments after he put the telephone down, we had our new Padrons. It was the computer's fault, Vicente said. It appeared that we were unlucky enough to be the very first people to produce an apparently out-dated Residencia certificate, and his computer program had not been updated accordingly.

He waved us off wreathed in smiles, as if it had never taken us two weeks of battling too and fro to get a standard form. But that's Spain for you! And the moral of the story? Don´t worry about it too much, just smile and keep on trying. Eventually, the ball of wool will become untangled, and you'll know better next time!

Please, do not let this sort of thing put you off retiring here. I hope that with the aid of this guide, you will find the path much, much smoother than we did. It's definitely a case of "If only I knew then what I know now!"

The Costa Blanca must be one of the most beautiful places it is possible to retire to. Before we moved over, everybody said the same thing "You'll be ever so bored, you know. What are you going to do with yourselves all day?" I can say, hand on heart, we haven't had time to be bored. Never forget, you are moving here to live, not to holiday, and that is two very different things.

We love it here, and I hope that you will, as well. Ask the right questions, be sure the move is right for you, and I know that you will.

Chapter 1

Before you Leap …..

Congratulations on making it this far! You are obviously serious about making the move to the lovely Costa Blanca. And why not? We Brits can't get enough of it. Millions of us holiday here every year, and thousands of us decide to live here. It is an exceptionally beautiful place to live. But before we move on to the hows and whys of moving to the Costa Blanca, first … a few prior thoughts that you may find interesting.

To begin – where exactly *is* the Costa Blanca? It stretches for some 200km along Spain's Mediterranean coastline. Given that we Brits have such a long ongoing love affair with the area, it's perhaps not surprising that the term "Costa Blanca" ("White Coast") isn't even Spanish! It was actually coined by British European Airways (BEA) when they launched their first air flight service from Gatwick to Valencia, in 1957. And the cost? £38. 16s! In real terms, actually a lot more than it is now.

The Costa Blanca extends from the large (by Costa Blanca standards anyway) town of Denia in the north, to Pilar de la Horadada in the south. Beyond Denia, the coast becomes the Costa del Azahar; to the south of Pilar is the Costa Calida.

The Costa Blanca is generally viewed as two halves, and given the fairly short stretch it occupies; it is surprising how different the two areas areas are.

The Southern stretch is hotter, drier, browner, flatter and more intensively populated than the north. Generally (although, of course, there are always exceptions) centers of population in the South tend to be in towns, which are often sited alongside the beautiful beaches, or in very large urbanizations (see below), often clustered around golf courses. Because the South is very much a centre of tourism, you may well get away with speaking little or no Spanish in this area. A great advantage if you are thinking of moving to the Southern Costa Blanca is the fact that property here is much cheaper than in the North.

In contrast to the Southern Costa Blanca, the North of the area is very green. It is cooler than the South (although still very hot, with extremely mild winters). Populations tend to congregate in areas around towns, known as "urbanizations" (more or less equivalent to an English estate) or in smaller villages and towns. The geography is more mountainous than the South. Outside the main cities, it helps greatly if you can speak at least a little Spanish, although a smile and a little pleasantness still go a long way! It is also a great deal more expensive to buy property in this area.

I am, of course, prejudiced as I live in the Northern Costa Blanca, but to my mind the scenery is infinitely greener and more beautiful than the South, and the climate – whilst still very hot in summer – kinder, even in winter.

Generally, the North is less anglicized than the South, but even so there are an awful lot of us ex-pats here.

Within the Costa Blanca, North and South, there are towns and villages to suit all tastes. If you want noisy, bustling, cheap and cheerful, then try Benidorm (http://www.benidorm.org) or Torrieveja (www.torrieveja.com) For a quieter, more family orientated resort with plenty of bars and restaurants, but virtually no night clubs, try Javea (www.javea.com). For a real treat, try sitting on the long promenade at Javea, facing the sea, on a late Sunday afternoon. As you sip your wine, and munch on your tapas, watch the world go by, which in Java's case generally means watching Spanish family groups – Granddad and Grandma, Mum and Dad, and children varying from teens to toddlers, all dressed up in their Sunday best, and not an i-pod or mobile in sight – meandering slowly up and down, stopping for a chat every now and then, but generally just enjoying the walk and the weather. It really is a part of life that seems to have vanished in the UK, and is truly delightful to be part of.

Or for a touch of the real Spain, you can do no better than visit Gandia (to give it it's full name, Real de Gandia) with it's wonderful architecture and "strollable" centre (www.gandia.org) and don't forget to visit the Borgia's Palace. I bet you didn't even know the Borgia's were Spanish, did you? It goes without saying that all of these resorts have clean, wonderful beaches. In Denia's case, 22km of beaches, and all totally flat and accessible.

Go a very little way inland, and you will find – literally every couple of kilometers – villages and small towns where, suddenly, everything is very much more traditional Spanish. And very much cheaper than the coastal areas.

So much to choose from! It's a reasonable guess that if you're considering moving here that you've taken holidays in the area before. But please remember, *living* somewhere is entirely different from simply going on holiday. This is particularly the case if you've always stayed in a hotel, which means that at best you have been one removed from reality. It may well be that the very things that attracted you to the area for a holiday are the same things that you may hate to live with full time – think of the bustle, the tourists, the heat…

So, you've been to the same resort on the undeniably beautiful Costa Blanca for years. Possibly even stayed in the same hotel or aparthotel or apartment complex each time. You know the area well, and love it. Love the people, the climate, the way of life. And now that retirement is approaching, you feel that the time has come to up sticks and retire to live the dream. At this point ......
REPEAT AFTER ME, THIS IS NOT A HOLIDAY!!!

Apologies if I am stating the obvious; I'm not trying to be facetious. I have lived in Valencia for 8 wonderful years, and I love Spain, and in particular the Costa Blanca. I love the lifestyle, the people, the food and not least, the climate. If you really want to move here, then I wish you all the best and I am sure – with a lot of forward planning – you will be equally happy. But please, don't fall into the trap that catches so many people; at the risk of repeating myself, living here is totally different from **holidaying** here.

Think about it logically; you spend a lot of the year planning your holiday. You ensure that you have sufficient funds, that all your needs have been carefully covered. You know where you want to go, what you want to do when you arrive. Why should moving permanently need any less thought? You may be surprised how often this planning stage is simply forgotten in the urge to live the dream, particularly when it's snowing outside, there's nothing worth watching on TV and Monday means the start of yet another hectic week.

At this stage, take a step back, pick up a calculator and notepad, and start planning. Think before you leap, and the dream is there for the taking. Forget holidays and think living, happily, for the rest of your life. And also, don't forget the obvious things. From my own experiences, and those of friends, the absolute basics you need to think about at this stage (and don't worry about actually buying a property for a while, that comes a lot later) are:

MONEY – You have to eat. Pay taxes and council taxes (and if you don´t know what these are likely to be in the area where you want to live, find out – NOW), pay your heating – and cooling - bills. Basically, everything that you now spend in England will be duplicated in Spain, If you are going to live on a pension, rather than taking a wage home each month, then you will automatically have less money at your disposal. Think about what you are going to have to spend on a day-to-day basis, and plan what you are going to need to spend, carefully.

LOCATION – Do you really want to live in one of the tourist hotspots where you normally holiday? Sure you wouldn't prefer something a little quieter, where the nightlife doesn't rock and roll around you until the small hours? And don't forget, living in a town costs far more than settling in the surrounding areas. And it's an excellent idea, once you've found your place in the sun, to visit it more than once; a lot more than once! Check it out at different times of the day, to see how much sun you get on the terrace at different times. If at all possible, check it out at different times of the year. You never know, what looks wonderful in the height of summer might be a different story in winter, and vice versa. That nice, quiet village could become a seething mass of tourists in summer, and you could find a totally unexpected pavement café outside your window, or a market taking over the street every Sunday. Even if you fall in love with a property, don't let your heart rule your head and find yourself rushing into a decision you might regret later. Think of all the questions you would ask before you bought property in England, at the very, very least.

LANGUAGE – Don´t speak a word of Spanish? Never felt the need? Learn at least a few words, ASAP. Outside the main areas, not that many people speak English, and at the very least it helps to know what the labels on the packages in the shops mean! It´s either that, or worry whether that pack of beef steak is actually horse......If you´ve set your heart on Benidorm or Torrieveja, and are sure you are not going to spend any time outside these areas, then you will probably manage nicely without ever having to utter a word of Spanish. Move outside the totally English enclaves, and it´s no good expecting all the locals to speak English – they don´t. Spain is far, far less of a "nanny" state than the UK; official documents are in Castellan or Valenciano, not English. Most doctors speak a little English, but if your Spanish is less than fluent, you will be expected to take an interpreter along. The good thing is that you will be pleasantly surprised how quickly you pick up some conversational Spanish, if you are confident enough to try to speak a little to the locals. And don´t worry about sounding foolish; the Spanish are lovely, patient people. If you will only try a few words of Spanish, it doesn´t matter how badly pronounced they are – the person you are talking to will happily spend ages correcting you, and helping you learn a bit more.

LIFESTYLE – This covers a multitude of sins, but think about it carefully, especially if you've only holidayed in hotels. What type of accommodation do you want? An apartment may be fine for a holiday, but could you live there? Can you afford a villa with a pool, together with all the associated maintenance costs (you can, of course, learn to maintain it yourself, but you still need chemicals, and professional help if something goes wrong)? If you live outside the centre, you will need a car (most places do have a bus or tram service, but it can be erratic, and may not go exactly where you want) – are you confident to drive on the wrong side of the road? Happy that you fully understand Spanish driving regulations? What about shopping (and no, honestly, you cannot afford to eat out twice a day for the rest of your life) – are you happy to try local shops? Have a go at markets? Happy with coping with temperatures in excess of 40° centigrade for months on end? Nights where it doesn't fall below 25°? Certain you will be happy with Spanish food? And before you say "of course"... one of our neighbours bought a holiday home here a few years ago. They have just sold it, and taken a huge loss.

Why? They had holidayed in the area for years, and were sure that this area, and Spain itself, was for them. They had bought with the intention of retiring here, just as soon as the kids were off their hands. Speaking to them just before they moved their belongings back to the UK, the wife told me that they had made a terrible mistake. Or rather, a number of terrible mistakes.

Before buying, they had only ever holidayed in hotels in the area, and never in the scorching summer months. It turned out that her husband hated the heat (they couldn't afford to run the air conditioning for as long as they would have really liked, which was 24 hours per day); found out he didn't like Spanish food; couldn't be bothered to learn Spanish, and even decided he didn't like Spanish beer! Whilst she would have been happy to stay, the thought of retirement with a perpetually very unhappy partner had changed even her mind.

So, look – or rather think – before you leap.

WEATHER – Sure, our weather in Spain is wonderful – for most of the year. Unless you live in the mountains, you are unlikely to get snow or ice, but winter (especially once you've lived here for a while) is chilly, and you will need some form of heating. Sorry, it is NOT possible to sunbathe all year! Also, in the summer it gets very, very hot in both North and South. This is, of course, a wonderful bonus when you are on holiday, but after a couple of years you will, I promise you, be leaning very carefully on your garden railings (carefully, because the metal railings will blister your skin if you're not careful) chatting to your neighbours about how nice it would be to see a bit of rain… You no doubt insisted on air conditioning whilst you were here on holiday, and you will need it now as well. Only this time, of course, it's you who will be paying the bill for it.

The sun is for holidaymakers, the rest of us stay inside, or in the naya (a type of arched, open porch on the side of most traditional Spanish villas – think conservatory without glass) during the summer months, or if we venture out it's to sit in the shade of a parasol.

It's lovely, of course, but don't factor it in as a major aspect of wanting to move here. You **will** get used to it; you **will** start taking it for granted, and you **will** – please don't laugh – start longing for a really long, refreshing shower of rain. I promise you! However, the amusement value to be gained from watching the UK weather forecast never seems to lessen....

BUREAUCRACY – The real problem area. Spanish bureaucracy is much, much worse than England. Everything needs a form, and if you don't know the right question to ask, you will find yourself visiting the same office, time after time, clutching yet more paperwork, only to be greeted with a sad shake of the head and a request for something else that wasn't mentioned last time. Grit your teeth, smile and take an interpreter is my advice. It's worth living with, and I hope that this guide will make it a much easier process. I have tried to cover all the most difficult areas, and certainly all those that you are most likely to come across.

Wherever possible, I have given the website for the relevant area; more often than not, there is an English version available and if the website doesn´t cover the specific problem, there will be a contact link so you can get further information. If you´re still stuck, drop me an e-mail yvonnebartholomew@telitec.com. I can´t guarantee I can help, but I will certainly try, and at the very least it´s a comfort to have some sort of helpline hovering in the background.

Here's hoping you never need to get in touch, except to tell me how much you are enjoying your new life in Spain!

HOMESICKNESS – Hand on heart, something I´ve never suffered from – this is my home, here in Spain, and as the old saying has it, "home is where the heart is". But many, many people do miss what they have left behind – the Grandkids, the shops, the ability to speak and understand the language easily; even – believe it or not! – the weather. All these things tug at the heart strings, so think about it carefully. If you have a partner, it is **vital** that the decision to move is heartfelt on both sides. If one of you isn´t entirely sure, then quite simply, don´t do it!

For every couple that moves across to Spain, there is another couple – or more often, one half of that couple - desperately wanting to go back "home" to England. The reasons I've heard for wanting to go back vary from "I can't learn Spanish and I don't feel comfortable here" to "It's not what I expected" to (and you would be surprised how often this one comes up) "I don't want to die here!"

The ex-pat population seems to be divided into two distinct halves; those of us who love it here, and wouldn't move back to England for anything, and those who feel they have made a big mistake, and want to go back NOW!

Please be aware; if it isn't for you, then selling (particularly if you are not registered as a resident) is a long and expensive business. If you haven't lived here for some years, and are not registered for tax in Spain (more about all of that later) then make no mistake, you will lose money on the transaction. I'm not trying to put you off moving here, just trying to convince you that you must be absolutely sure before both of you makes the decision to move.

Even moving to a different city in the UK can be a major decision, and one that requires much thought. How much more thought, then, does moving to a different country, beginning a whole new lifestyle, require?

I know, it's only a short air trip away from England (and in the Costa Blanca we are lucky to be served by 2 excellent airports, 1 at Alicante and 1 at Valencia, so both parts of the Costa are well covered) and air flights are ridiculously cheap, especially if you can grab a bargain, but …. It's still a long way from "home". And if you are still thinking of England as "home", you may have problems.

RETIRING OR WORKING? - At present, (2014) unemployment is around 25% in the Costa Blanca area. This grim statistic should be enough to tell you that you are very unlikely to find work over here. You would be surprised how many people do "retire" here, assuming they will be able to find a nice, little job to supplement their income, just waiting for them as soon as they unpack.

Basically, forget it! You may be very lucky, and find a niche locally, perhaps working in an "English" bar, or cleaning villas for ex-pats who have a holiday home. But it´s far from guaranteed, and the competition for this sort of job is fierce. Even worse are those hapless souls who decide they will sell up in England, and use the proceeds to buy a business over here; more often than not, a bar or restaurant. For some strange reason, in the vast majority of cases this is done by people who have no experience whatsoever in running the particular business, and nor do they speak a word of Spanish. Think about it; if you were in England, what sort of success rate would you expect to achieve if you bought a pub, never having even served behind a bar in your life? Exactly. But people will persist in doing it, having no idea how to make the business a success, no idea of the paperwork involved, no idea how many customers they are likely to get, no idea of the competition, even without a thought as to why the business was for sale in the first place......If you must do it, *please* think carefully about everything that is involved first.

Ideally, before you make your decision, I would advise hiring a villa or apartment in the area you want to live in, for at least a month. If you can manage it for longer, then so much the better. Get the feel of living here, rather than holidaying. Haunt the estate agents, and ask them all the questions you would if you were moving to a different area in England. Read the local papers. Talk to your neighbours. Keep an eye on your budget. If it isn't what you expected, or what you hoped, then you have had an excellent holiday and have lost nothing. If it lives up to expectations, you've got a superb base to start your planning. And there has not been a better time to buy for years; there is plenty of housing stock available, from apartments to luxury villas, and many ex-pats (of all nationalities) are keen to sell. The Brits are selling for the reasons I've already discussed. Many Germans were forced to put their homes on the market a few years ago, when the tax man started to ask awkward questions and they had to sell to pay the bill. You may well find that you can scoop up an absolute bargain; sometimes homes come literally completely furnished – down to the last teaspoon! But be warned, don't buy in a hurry. Take your time and make sure that your dream is reality, rather than a nightmare.

Chapter 2

The Buying Process – Legal Aspects

Even if you have bought and sold properties umpteen times in England, you'll quickly find that it bears very little resemblance to the process in Spain.

As soon as you have decided that you definitely want to take the plunge and buy, either for a holiday home initially, or to retire to at once, you must do 3 things. Before you even set foot in an Estate Agent! You **must** do these before you even think about making an offer on a property, or you will not even get past the starting post.

In order of importance, these are:

Obtain an NIE number

Open a Spanish bank account

Ensure you have enough money ready to pay deposits, first stage payments etc – preferably in your Spanish bank account

Firstly, and most importantly, you have to acquire (or if you have a partner, both of you have to acquire) an **NIE number**. This is roughly equivalent to an English National Insurance number, but far more important in daily life in Spain. If you buy a gas cylinder, you will be asked for your NIE. If you buy a major electrical appliance, or a car, you will be asked for your NIE. If you have to sign for a letter at the Correos (Post Office) … you guessed it, you will be asked for your NIE number. Until you learn it off by heart, keep it in your diary or address book. Sometimes you can get away with giving your passport number (and incidentally, you should always carry your passport with you. You can get away with getting it copied and reduced to credit card size, and most photo shops will laminate it for you as well, for a couple of euros. But you do need at least a copy with you, always. It´s a legal requirement not only for you to have a current passport, but to have a copy with you. See? Something else you´ve learned!) but not always. Sometimes, only an NIE number will do, and this is certainly the case when you are buying property. Only foreigners who have property in Spain need an NIE, the Spanish themselves have another form of ID number.

So, how do you get one? There are 2 ways. You can apply in person, if you are feeling confident and have a bit of time, by going to your nearest Guardia Civil Station which has a Foreigners Department ("Departmento de Extranjeros"). These are generally located in the larger cities – e.g. Denia, Benidorm and Alicante, and I would strongly advise you to check in advance if you need an appointment – most do, and will not budge if you haven't got one. To find your nearest Office, either check Pagos Amarillos (Yellow Pages) or go on line. I can't give you a direct link, as each office has it's own administration. It's also a good idea to take an interpreter with you, as – no disrespect intended – your average Guardia Civil is unlikely to speak the wide range of foreign languages he's going to meet in a working day. Also, the forms are all in Spanish.

You will need to take with you the following:

Your original passport, together with a photocopy
2 passport sized photographs of yourself*

*You can get the photographs done in the automatic booths you find outside supermarkets, etc. But they do have to be a regulation size, so check carefully on the booth to find which one you want. It's very little more expensive to go to a photographer in your local town, and tell them what you want the photographs for – that way you are sure you get the right size.

Once you have completed your form, they will give you a copy of it, and also return your original passport. It will then take anywhere between a couple of days and a couple of weeks to process your application. If you are in Spain during this time, give the Guardia a telephone number (yours, or your interpreter) to contact you. If not, give them a contact address – preferably someone who can pick your NIE up when it´s ready – if it stays with the Guardia for months, it could disappear and you would have to start the process all over again.

You need to collect the NIE certificate in person with your passport and the copy given to you; if you can´t do this, you must give a letter of authorization (in Spanish) to your representative to allow them to pick it up for you. The certificate is a stamped, white A4 size paper document with your name and NIE number. Once you have it, keep it in a safe place! If you lose it and have not got a record of the number, you will have to start the process all over again and the Guardia are unlikely to be impressed.

If you would prefer – and personally this is the route I would take – you can pay somebody what is usually a very reasonable sum to sort the paperwork and go with you to obtain the NIE, and also pick it up for you. (At the time of writing, around €130 + IVA). Your Accountant (haven´t got one yet? Get one! I´ll explain why later) or your Abogado (solicitor) can do it for you, or there are a number of firms who offer this service - easy to find either on line, or via advertisements in the local papers.

Once you have your NIE – and not before – you can actually consider buying property. But before you actually do this, you will need to **open a Spanish bank account.** Why? Because you will need sufficient funds to hand to pay for deposits, possibly fees to take your selected property off the market, stage payments, fees for your Abogado, fees for the Notary and all the other bits and pieces that start to build up as soon as you have decided to buy. Once opened, you will have a cheque book, debit card and – if you want it – a credit card. Remember, it can take a period from a few days to weeks to make a transfer from a UK bank to somebody else's account, and the last thing you want at this stage is to worry about whether large sums of money have vanished in transit. If you have a Spanish account, this problem vanishes. There used to be a number of British banks active in Spain, but these now seem to have shrunk, since Lloyds sold their Spanish banking concern to Sabadell, to Santander and Barclay's, and ING Direct online. You don't, of course, have to use a British bank – there are many large Spanish banks available, but it is well worth shopping around and – literally! – having a look at Spanish bank premises to see if they have a notice in the window to say they speak English. We have 2 Spanish bank accounts, and they are both exemplary. Only one small niggle; all Spanish banks still charge you fees for using them. You can cut down on these by asking for internet statements only, but you will still get quarterly charges and hefty administration fees if you go overdrawn. Even worse, you will probably find that if you don't have enough money in your account to meet bills, then those bills will simply not be paid, which in turn causes huge problems putting things right.

Nor do you have to use your British bank account to make transfers to Spain. There are a number of companies who offer very good exchange rates at low cost (not being in the business of advertising such concerns, I suggest you take a look in either the Costa Blanca News or any "free" paper for a selection), but you must remember to add an extra day or two to transfers if you are using an intermediary.

Having opened your Spanish bank account (and it really is very easy – take your passport with you, and your all important NIE number) remember to put **sufficient money into it to cover any expenses that may arise in purchasing your property, together with, say, 10% extra for contingencies and unforeseen costs.** Some people take extra cash with them, and literally pay it into their account personally. Others do a bank-to-bank transfer, or use an intermediary to make the transfer at an agreed currency rate. If you use either of the latter to keep your Spanish account healthy, you will need **your Spanish account number, the full address of the bank, your BIC/SWIFT identifier and your IBAN number.** When you open your Spanish account, ask your new bank for all these details as finding them afterwards can be a time consuming task. It is fiddly setting up the transfer details initially, but you only have to do it once. I would also strongly urge you to ask your Spanish bank to set up online banking for your account. This way, you can check the account balance even if you are in England, and make sure that all your direct debits have been paid correctly. And if problems arise, you can instantly print off a statement to wave under the noses of whoever is demanding more money off you!

So, you have done the **3 Golden Rules**. You have an NIE. You have opened a Spanish bank account, and there is money in it. Where do you go from here? At some point in the near future, you will have to appoint an Abogado to undertake the conveyancing for you.

Unlike the UK, it is legal in Spain for the same Abogado to work for you, and the person or company you are buying the property from. Personally, I am not enchanted by this idea. It might look good on paper, and your Developer may well try and sell it to you as a way of saving costs – after all, the same Abogado is working for both of you, so it must be cheaper and quicker – but in the real world, you will use the Abogado once, whereas your Developer may well have developed a nice, cosy relationship with him over a number of years. It is also, of course, tempting in that it saves you the chore of finding an Abogado in Spain, but I would strongly advise against it. It's quite easy to check the local newspaper for Abogados in your area, or you can do a search online. Even better – ask your potential neighbours who they used, and if they were happy with the service. You need an Abogado who speaks English, of course, and it's a great help if you can find one who is online, as it will be easier to contact them before you move over. If you give your Abogado your budget for your property purchase, they should be able to give you a fairly concise estimate of what sort of fees you will be facing for the purchase. Welll worth remembering; whatever your budget is, **add 10%** to it. This will cover purchase tax (8%) and the legal fees for your Abogado and Notary.

Both buying and selling property in Spain is best described as an interesting process! Generally, the paperwork is completely different to that in England, and also – perhaps surprisingly – the process can be a great deal quicker, especially if you are buying a second-hand or already completed property.

You've probably seen headlines in the local press about ex-pats who have bought, only to find their property is illegal and is about to be demolished. Even worse, people who have turned up with their pockets bulging with cash ready to buy, and who have been mugged or even murdered. Please, bear in mind the reason that this sort of thing makes the headlines in the first place is because it's unusual, and hence news. Do your research first, and it isn't going to happen to you.

I would never advise buying Spanish property at auction, but if you must do it, DO NOT, under any circumstances, carry your purchase money about with you. And never, ever, talk to strangers in bars about your plans. Of course you wouldn't be so silly; but some people are, and have been murdered for their cash as a result. It could happen anywhere, so make sure it´s doesn´t happen to you!

Moving on, before I discuss the buying routes open to you, I want to explain the actual *process.*

You have seen the property of your dreams, and are ready to purchase. So what happens now? To begin with, make sure you have enough money ready! Unlike England, you need to be aware that **there are no property chains in Spain.**

This aspect takes a bit of getting your head around.

The reason there are no chains is simple – if you want to buy property in Spain, you are either a first-time buyer with a mortgage offer in place or – if you are really lucky – sufficient money in the bank already to hand. Or **you have already sold your own property.** Or again, are lucky enough to have money ready. The point I am making is that it's the other way around to the UK, where you find a house you like and then put your own property on the market. In Spain, you sell first and then start looking! One of the first question house sellers are likely to ask is; "Have you sold your own house?" If the answer is "No" they are likely to assume you are just a "looker" rather than a serious purchaser. In this case, you will probably find that they are really not very interested in negotiating, as everybody expects buyers to be ready to proceed now, not at some undefined period in the future. Nice not to have a chain, though, but this is also something to bear in mind for the future, if and when you want to sell your own house in Spain.

You may be lucky, and find a vendor who is willing to take their property off the market until you have your funds sorted out, but this is far from guaranteed. If they will do this, then you will be expected to make a deposit (usually €3000) and beware; if you change your mind and decide not to buy, unless there is a legal reason for not doing so (for instance, you find the Escritura is not available, or the property is an illegal build) this deposit is not refundable.

Occasionally, you may find a vendor who is willing to **rent** the property to you initially, to see if you really like it. If this happens, any rent you pay in the first year is usually deductible from the final purchase price, with each succeeding year (normally up to a maximum of 3 years) refundable on a sliding scale.

Assuming that you do not want to rent, and are in a position to proceed immediately once negotiations are complete, then you will be expected to put down a deposit, literally as soon as you can get to the bank. The deposit on a second hand property is normally 10% of the agreed asking price. This is paid to the Estate Agent, if your vendor is using one, or to their Abogado if they are not. Again, beware! If you back out of the purchase for other than legal reasons, you must forfeit your deposit.

Once the deposit is paid, a completion date is agreed between your and your vendor. This is very much a matter of agreement, but if you are both happy, it can be a surprisingly quick process. Once the completion day is agreed, your Abogado will make an appointment at the Notary for you and your vendor. The Notary is best defined as a para-legal, and it is the Notary who will draw up the Escritura ("Deeds") for you, and actually arrange the transfer of the property from the vendor, to you. You both attend, sign on the dotted line, and you hand over the rest of the purchase price.

If it's impossible for you to get over on the due date, it's not a problem. You can give your Abogado power of attorney to act on your behalf – but make sure the power of attorney is carefully worded so that this is the only action they have – and he or she will go to the Notary and sign on your behalf.

At this stage, a word about "black" money may be in order. Never heard of it? Well, to start with, it's illegal. And it's not supposed to happen these days. But it does!

The way it works is this:

You have agreed to buy Juan's villa for the sum of €100,000. Both of you will incur taxes on the sale. However, Juan has proposed that you tell the Abogado and the Notary that the actual cost of the villa is €80,000, which cuts the tax bill down for both of you. If you agree, this will be sum that appears on your Escritura and all the other legal documents.

So when you both arrive at the Notary, Juan has a quiet word with the official, and when the time arrives for the money to be handed over, the Notary suddenly discovers he has to leave the room for a moment or two, and in his absence you hand Juan a brown envelope bulging with euros. Lovely! You've both saved money, and nobody is going to tell the taxman, are they?

In practice, it may not all be plain sailing. To start with, it *is* illegal, and the Hacienda (Tax Office) is getting very excited about this sort of dodge. Also, you may find yourself with a demand for a "plus valia" (more about this later) at some point further down the line.

However, assuming all goes well the villa is now yours! It may be a little surprising at first, but it is quite customary for you to own your new property, but still agree to the vendor living there for a while longer, or storing furniture in it. It's not in any way a legal agreement, but it does happen quite often. If you're not in a hurry to move in yourself, it does have the distinct advantage of keeping the property inhabited.

If you're buying new build (i.e. you are buying a plot and having a property built on it), the process is different again. You will be expected to make a deposit (usually 10%) as soon as you reserve your plot. You will then make stage payments (normally after the foundations are laid; when the walls are up; and when the roof is on) together with a final payment when you have viewed the property on completion, and are satisfied with it.

All the stage payment dates should be agreed up front, so you don´t get any nasty shocks. If your Developer rings up out of the blue and tells you the roof has just gone on, 3 months ahead of schedule, tell him firmly that that is his problem, not yours; you don´t have to pay early.

Again, you must have an Abogado, and you will have to visit (or get your Abogado to do it for you) the Notary to complete the transaction.

Chapter 3

The Buying Process – The Practical Bits!

So that's the legal process sorted out; you know what to expect, and what taxes and expenses you will have to pay. But how do you actually go about finding that all important dream property on the Costa Blanca? The first decision is whether to go for new build, or second hand ("pre-owned" to use the Estate Agents jargon).

A few years ago, at the height of the housing boom in Spain, many English buyers bought new property. This was purchased either "off plan" or was bespoke build. Off plan went out of favour for a number of reasons; basically, a developer bought a large plot of land, decided what he wanted to build on it, and then started building. Purchasers bought a specific plot, with a specific type of property on it. Stage payments were made as the build progressed.

Unfortunately, some builders went bankrupt before houses were finished, and a number of schemes were promoted that enticed people to buy, with a view to selling before completion and making a profit in the process. With the collapse of the new housing market, prices went down and buyers found themselves saddled with a house with negative equity.

Hardly surprisingly, this type of real estate selling has gone out of favour since the housing boom collapsed, and there is now a variety of housing stock on the market at very reasonable prices. However, recently "off plan" has reared its head again, now the property market is picking up.

If you want to buy off plan, then there are a number of things you must be aware of.

Firstly, check out your Developer.

Have you heard of them? Can they give you references from satisfied purchasers? How big are they? Although it must be said that "huge" is not necessarily a watertight safeguard – FADESA, who were not only one of the biggest companies in Spain, but also owned part of British Airports, went into voluntary liquidation a few years ago, mainly as a result of over-reaching themselves in the housing market. All credit to FADESA, however, as soon as they could, they offered everybody who had bought an off plan – and unfinished – property from them the choice of their money back, or waiting and getting the property finished.

If possible, take a good look at completed property, so you can get a feel of finish standard. If people are in residence, see if you can have a chat to them, to get a better idea of any problem areas.

If the site has not been developed at all, ask if the Developer actually has all planning permissions in place. If the answer is "pending", then think twice before paying out any money in deposits.

You may think it's a given that planning consents will be in place, but it's worth considering that a few years ago a very large, very well known English Developer advertised a new development in Murcia – in fact, spent a fortune advertising it – and sold quite a few properties, only to discover that the local council were not prepared to grant the relevant planning permissions. Oops!

Admittedly, the Developer did offer refunds of the deposits, or property elsewhere but that still didn't resolve the fact that quite a lot of people where not getting the home that they wanted, in the location they had set their hearts on!

It is a legal requirement in Spain that if you are buying a new property, and are making stage payments then your Developer **must** have taken out a bank guarantee to cover his debts in the even that he goes bankrupt. Ensure that this is in place, and is, preferably, with one of the bigger banks.

Spain has a multitude of small, local banks, and in the past few years a number of these have gone under, often as a result of over extending themselves in the mortgage market. Your Abogado will ensure that this is in place for you. Some Developers have been know to try and tell you that a Bank Guarantee isn´t necessary, as you are making stage payments so will only pay the value of the work done. Don´t listen to them! You are entitled to a Bank Guarantee, and you need it.

You should also be aware of the timescale for completion for off-plan property. If you choose a plot that is right at the end of the build, then you could be waiting several years for completion. On the other hand, if your plot is next in line for construction, make sure you have funds to hand. And don´t forget – in this case, you are likely to be living on a building site until completion of the whole estate!

Also worth considering is the fact that it is a legal requirement for every new property to come with a 10-year builder's guarantee. Don´t let your Developer fool you by making this a selling point; he hasn't got any choice in the matter.

On the other hand, if you want a new property, but don't fancy buying off plan, you have further choices. You are still quite likely to come across property that is a couple of years old, but has never been sold. These really can be a bargain, as Developers want to get them off their hands. But bear in mind that what you see is what you get – you will not be able to customize the property in any way, and if it has been standing empty for some times, it may have issues with damp or could come complete with original defects, rather than original features.

You can also invest in a new, "one off" property, built either entirely to your specification or – a much cheaper option – built to a standard developer's design, but modified to suit you. New property is generally on an existing Urbanization, in which case you will choose your plot and discuss the model of property you want with the Developer, asking him to make any changes you want to the standard model, or you will normally have the option of asking the Developer to design and build a property exactly to your specification. The latter option, of course, being the most expensive.

If you want an individual plot, which is not on a developed Urbanization, it can be done but is a far more complex option; you will have to source the land, ensure that planning permission for what you want to build will be granted (and don´t believe the Estate Agent when they inform you breezily that the plot has a ruin on it, and so of course you can build with no problems. It ain´t necessarily so!), and then either employ an architect to draw up plans and get your permissions and a builder to do the work, or find a Developer who will do everything for you.

If you are going down this route, either you or your Developer **must** have an architect; it´s not only a legal requirement, but it´s also for your own protection. In practice, it´s easier and safer to get either a Developer or a builder who also employs an architect and take the build as a package, or an architect who also has a building company and again offers a package. I realise this may not sound sensible; surely, it would be better to employ an independent architect, who would safeguard your interests? In principle, yes. In practice, the answer is often "No."

Let me explain. You have an independent architect, who collaborates with you to design your dream home. That architect will also supervise the builder, whom you have chosen, and who has no legal relationship with the architect. If everything goes according to plan, then absolutely fine. But if something goes wrong – say the builder doesn't comply with your timescale, or the standard of workmanship isn't what you expected – then problems start to loom. Both parties are likely to point the finger of blame at the other; the builder will insist he followed the architects' instructions, so it's not his fault. The architect, of course, will deny this and say it's *your* builder who has made a mess of things. Stalemate. And of course, you're stuck in the UK, unable to move things along as you would wish. You may, of course, decide to resort to the Courts to sort things out for you. There is nothing wrong with the Spanish judicial system, other than the fact that is very, very slow – the average wait for a court case to be heard is around 3 years! And unlike the English system, you are unlikely to know much about the process.

Still not convinced? Let me give you a real-life example. My very good friend, lets call him James, decided to buy a villa in Calpe. He bought a plot, but wanted an individual house, so employed an architect to draw up the designs. The local Developer agreed to undertake the build. Alas, the Developer was over-extended and went bankrupt a quarter of the way through the build. James had made stage payments, so was not out of pocket, but as he was in the UK he readily agreed to allow his architect to find him a builder to finish the work. All appeared to go well, apart from the luxurious swimming pool, which was to have been a feature of the villa. When James arrived to make his final inspection, he found the pool was not at all what he had expected – it was in the right place, but was far smaller than he had specified, and did not have the Roman steps he had asked for. He pointed this out to the architect, who shrugged. Not his problem, he said. The work had been done by James´ original builder. He, the architect, had of course made sure the work was done to the correct standard, as far as possible. In fact, he was certain that he had mentioned the possible problem to James at some point. Did James want the new builder to make changes? This would, of course, be costly and would take time, but it could be done.

James, of course, was far from happy. He insisted that it was the architect's responsibility to ensure the build was done according to plan. The architect insisted he had done all he could, and that the problem lay with the original builder. As I type, the case is waiting to go to Court, but I'm not holding my breath over the outcome. And the really sad thing is that I just cannot convince James that things do not happen in Spain in the way that they do in England. He says he has a watertight (if you'll forgive the pun) case, and that's it. We'll see....

So, the final decision on your build is up to you. It's unlikely that anything will go wrong, but as you will be far removed from the scene of the action, it's wise to be prepared as far as possible. The more you know, the more you plan, the less hassle you are going to get.

Generally, if you are going for new build in any shape or form, as with buying off-plan, you will make stage payments and will also get a 10-year guarantee on the property upon completion.

And penultimately, as far as you can, check potential running costs. Although you will have no idea of electricity and water consumption, your Developer should be able to tell you how much your IBI payments (the Spanish equivalent of Council Tax) will be, and whether you have to pay extra for "basura" (rubbish collection).

For new build, it´s perfectly normal for you to be on "Developer's electricity" and "Developer's water" for some time. Even years, if you're really lucky. In practice, this means that you do not have a contract with either Iberdrola or your local water company initially, but instead the Developer pays your utility bills. The period involved varies from months to years, but you should get sufficient warning before you switch to paying yourself.

Ask your Developer for your contract for both electric and water when you take them over; the electricity contract is particularly important as you will need this as and when you come to sell.

If you **are** buying new build, make sure you know what you are getting. Boundary walls may be included, but they are often an extra, as is landscaping. Air conditioning is unlikely to be standard, but you may well find that something called "pre-installation" is. In practice, this means that you will find a bundle of wires sticking out of the wall, waiting for an air-conditioning unit to be affixed. You still have to buy the units, and get somebody to install them for you, but it does mean that all your lovely new plaster doesn't have to be hacked away for the installation. You may be given the choice of having an open fireplace "as is" or one that is ready to receive a cassette. The "cassette" is actually the Spanish version of a glassed-in log burner, and very nice they are to! You still have to buy and install the log burner, but the process is cheaper and easier if you ask for the cassette version. On all new builds, you should be given a choice of tiles and finishes. Depending on the standard of finish of your villa (ranging from "standard" to "luxury") you will be offered a choice of tiles – the usual process is to take you to the tile manufacturers and show you the range of tiles that is available to you. The salesman will inevitably try to persuade you to opt for a more expensive type of tile, but if you like what's on offer in the "included" range, stand your ground.

On the question of "extras" it's a given that your Developer will be keen to sell you that bit more than is on offer on the standard model. Central heating, perhaps. Or a nice set of patio doors leading out of the master bedroom. Or what about Roman steps for your pool, rather than an aluminium ladder? Or perhaps you would like your Developer to actually install the air conditioning for you? After all, you are miles away in the UK, and of course it's much less hassle if you get it all done in the first place…well, yes, but don't forget this is all going to come at a cost. If you want to accept extras, don't just accept the Developers price. There's nothing to stop you from asking for a couple of quotes from independent companies, and if you're armed with these, you can use them to barter the Developer's price down.

I would advise taking the viewpoint that *if* you're sure you want it, then consider the Developer for structural extras. Obviously, Roman steps in the pool or a patio door will be messy and probably more expensive if you have it done later. But if it's not structural, and it can wait until you are in residence, then wait! If you're actually there, you can shop around for good prices and can keep an eye on the construction. Take advantage of bargain offers as well – keep an eye on the local papers for these.

Apologies for ranting on about new build at such length. We bought new, from a Developer, ourselves, and were very fortunate in that all our problems were little ones. Until we came to add on an extension, but that's a story for later! But I would still have been very, very grateful for the knowledge I now have.

Moving on to buying second hand property. At the moment, with such a lot of excellent property on the market, I would seriously advise you to look at this option. Generally, it will be cheaper than new build, but of course does have the disadvantage that you cannot specify exactly what you want. If the property is under 10 years old, you should get the balance of the builder's 10 year guarantee. And please, don't let anybody tell you that there is no such thing as a structural survey in Spain – there are a number of companies who offer this service, and although it is not a legal requirement to have a survey, I would strongly advise getting one. Would you buy a house in England without getting a survey first? Exactly! And of course, you will be expected to make full payment on completion, rather than spreading the cost via stage payments.

What else do you need to be aware of?

Firstly, the cost of the property. Because you can´t change it to suit your tastes, turn this to your advantage. You can use virtually anything as a bargaining point. At the moment, it´s a buyers´ market, so haggle. I suggest making a point of asking the Estate Agent or the Vendor how long the house has been on the market – the longer it is, then the more likely you are to get a reduction in the price. Even if it´s perfect, it´s also perfectly reasonable to try for at least a 5% discount.

Are you paying cash, rather than having to arrange a mortgage? Another great bargaining position! Speaking of bargaining ploys, it´s well worth looking out for home made "Se Vende" signs. You can´t miss these – they are generally luminous red or yellow, and will be pre-printed with the words "Se Vende" and have a telephone and/or mobile number on them. "Se Vende" is Spanish for "For Sale by Owner" and indicates that the owner is either selling themselves, without involving an Estate Agent in the process, or is willing to sell privately as well. Why is this a good sign? Because if it´s a private sale, the price should be lower in the first place. Bear in mind that Estate Agents in Spain generally charge fees of between 5 and 10% of the selling price, and a private sale should reflect this saving. And you can still practice your haggling skills…..

Once you´ve started looking around, you will probably have a very good idea of the areas you want to live in. Check out the local Estate Agents (a web search will find you literally dozens); they will be only too delighted to show you as many properties that they have on their books that are within your price range. As you go around with them, you will also get the chance to make a note of any suitable "Se Vende" properties.

There are also bargains to be had in bank repossessions, and auctions. But both do have their drawbacks.

Bank repossessions are often heavily discounted, because the bank simply wants its money back. But if you are buying a repossessed property, please, be very, very careful. You Abogado must ensure that all outstanding debts will be cleared by the sale; otherwise you could find that you have paid the asking price, but have also become saddled with an existing mortgage, or are responsible for other outstanding debts that come with the property. Buyer beware!

Auctions are another kettle of fish altogether. Offhand, I can't think of a single reason why I would recommend buying a Spanish property at auction.

They may well be cheap, but there is always a reason for that. Often, auction properties are in a very run down condition. They may also have bad debts attached to them. And of course, everything is done in a hurry, so you're unlikely to have time to get the "legal pack" translated properly. And once the hammer goes down, you have bought that property, and you cannot back out. And yes, if you simply try vanishing back to the UK, the Courts will find you, eventually.

And finally in this section, just why have I been banging on about the advantages of getting a good accountant?

Quite simply, they are worth their weight in gold! Expect to pay around €100 (+IVA) per year for their services.

For this, you can expect then to set up your direct debits for you (and change them as necessary – for instance, if you buy a new car, they will cancel your old Road Tax direct debit, and set up a new one for you); complete your tax return to the Hacienda; keep you informed of any new legislation that effects you; make your Form 720 submission (this is explained later, in the chapter on Taxes), and generally help out in a crisis.

To give you a very personal example; we have always paid our IBI (Council Tax) by direct debit. As a result, I was stunned to get a demand for an additional €1600! I dug out my bank statements and went to our local SUMA offices (more on SUMA later) and explained that there had surely been a mistake: here were the bills, and here the statements to say they had been paid. SUMA was not impressed.

I would have to fill out a form, they said (one thing you will find quickly in Spain, there is *always* a form), and then pay the €1600. Eventually, they would refund the money, once they had satisfied themselves that I had paid the right amount.

And they would not budge! I knew perfectly well if I handed over the €1600 it would take forever to get a refund, so asked my accountant if they could help. They marched down to SUMA and went through it all again with them, and filled in the relevant form for me. It turned out that SUMA had undercharged me slightly for the last 3 years, and that the total amount actually owing was … .€35.60! The original demand was for 3 years IBI, rather than the amount actually owed. I paid my €35.60 on line, and bought my accountant a box of chocolates.

Chapter 4

What you Need to Ask Before Buying

As I keep saying – and honestly, it cannot be said enough, because it is vital to understand it - buying property in Spain is completely different from buying in the UK. You´ve probably heard the expression "Spanish customs"? Well, it could well originate here!

Although your Abogado will check all the legal issues are in place, this doesn´t mean that you can´t ask questions – lots of questions - yourself. It makes sense – think of the disappointment and waste of time and effort if you find your dream home has major legal issues, that mean you no longer want to buy. There are also a lot of important but not necessarily deal breaking issues that you might want to think about.

I suggest making yourself a check-list of questions, and asking them at every viewing. It also has the advantage of letting your potential vendor know that you are on the ball, and could come in very useful as a bargaining tool.

The following issues are **essential,** and you must be certain about them before you buy.

Cedula – Yet another certificate, I´m afraid, but one that you need. The Cedula is the certificate of first habitation, and is issued by the local Council when, and only when, they are satisfied that the property has been completed to the correct standard, and is literally fit for habitation. Very occasionally, you may find that a Cedula has not been issued because the Council has a grouch with the Developer, rather than the property; if this is the case, you may want to go ahead without the Cedula, but get your Abogado to discuss the matter with the Council first. If the Cedula hasn't been issued because the property isn´t up to standard, do not buy.

Always ask if the property has a Cedula, and if not, why not!

Escritura – This is the legal document that tells you all you need to know about the property; it is the Spanish equivalent of the Deeds. If your vendor doesn´t have an Escritura, then alarm bells should start ringing, as they are normally issued very quickly after the property is bought initially, or on completion when it changes hands. In my days with the local Vecinos, I came across a very sad case where an English couple had bough their new villa directly from the Developer. He kept promising that their Escritura would be with them soon, but it never arrived.

After several years elapsed, the couple were considering selling their villa, and asked their Abogado to contact the Developer to demand the Escritura. At this stage, the Abogado discovered that the Developer could not produce the Escritura because he had actually taken out a mortgage on the land the villa was built on himself, and hence the Escritura was with the bank! And why didn´t the original Abogado find this out? Perhaps he did, but as he was acting for both the Developer and the purchaser, he somehow forgot to mention it. Sadly, the case is now going to court for resolution.

Iberdrola Electricity Connection – make sure your vendor (the **vendor, not the Developer)** has a contract with Iberdrola. I know this sounds strange, but it is normal for new build property to be on what is called "Developer's electricity" (i.e. the Developer pays for the electric, not you) for some time. Iberdrola will only enter into a formal contract with the householder when the electric connection is certified as correct. If the property is more than, at most, a couple of years old and still on Developer's electricity, then something is wrong. Although the Cedula is important, in real life if your vendor can produce the Escritura, and has a contract with Iberdrola, then you should be reasonably happy.

Planning Permissions – I will talk about planning permissions at some length later, but at this stage it's important to establish that if your vendor has had any construction work done on the house, all necessary planning permissions are in place. If they are not, then at some point in the future the Council could ask you to get the permissions, and pay for them.

In very extreme circumstances, you may find that the vendor has not applied for planning permission simply because he knew it would be refused. If this is a major issue, the Council could demand that the work be demolished. At the very least, they will refuse to issue a Cedula. Ever.

And please don´t believe people who tell you that permission is deemed to have been given if the Council doesn´t catch up on it within a six year period, and after this time limit they can´t do anything. It´s actually a **fourteen** year statute of limitation, and in any event, you really do not need the hassle.

Any major work should also appear on your Escritura. It doesn´t always happen, and if it isn´t done you may want to ask your vendor to get it put right before you go to the Notary.

Outstanding Debts – I know, rather difficult to ask this one tactfully, so you may wish to leave it to your Abogado. Suffice it to say that if there are any outstanding debts on the property (unpaid utility/IBI bills are a favourite) then they will devolve to you when you buy.

Utilities – Check to see if all utilities are connected. It´s relatively uncommon to have mains gas on the Costa Blanca, but properties normally have mains electricity, drainage and water supplies. You may well find that drainage is an issue, so ask if the property has mains drainage or a septic tank. If the latter, ask who is responsible for emptying it (it may be the Developer) – if it´s your problem, ask when it was last emptied, and how much it cost.

A small note of caution regarding utilities. Rural – particularly rural and isolated – property is quite likely to have a generator rather than mains electricity, and a septic tank rather than mains drainage. If you're happy with that, fine. Worth finding out how much it would cost for connections, but in any event do check to see what is connected, and in particular double check the water situation!

I heard recently of somebody who bought an exquisite Casa Rural (country house) at a bargain price.

The vendor told him, very honestly, that it did not have mains water, but water was supplied from a local orange grower, who had a perpetual water deposit. The water was cheap, and perfectly drinkable, so he went ahead happily and bought. Strangely, after a while he noticed that whenever it rained, he had no water at all. Not a drop. Puzzled, he asked the orange grower what the problem was. Oh, he replied, didn´t Signor Smith explain it to you? When it rains, I don´t have to irrigate my oranges, so your water supply is automatically cut off as well ....!

Energy Certificate – Anybody who is selling a property in Spain has to have one to give to the buyer. It shows you the energy rating of the house – i.e. how energy efficient it is. Generally, unless you're buying an eco-house, which is designed to be energy efficient, the rating will be a disappointing "f" or "g". It appears Spanish houses have too many windows, and air conditioning is not good for the environment.

And that's the end of the list for legal "must have´s". However, there are also a number of areas which fall into the "nice to know" category, and which could also be useful as bargaining ploys to get that all important price reduction.

In case you were wondering where it is, I have devoted an entire chapter to "Land Grab" which is less of a contentious issue than it was a few years ago, but is a factor you will want to bear in mind.

Worth checking on are the following:

Restrictive Covenants – or at least, the Spanish equivalents! These are often imposed by the local Council, and are well worth checking out. For instance, on our Urbanization, stone balustrades are outlawed. You are also not allowed to paint your house any colour other than white. Why? Because when permission was granted to the Developer to build in the first place, the planning permission was given for a "white" urbanization, with metal railings throughout. These are trivialities, but other areas can be more serious.

A case was highlighted in the local press recently regarding an apartment block which had been re-classified as an Aparthotel after application by the new management committee.

The case is complicated, but the gist of the problem is that existing residents, who have lived full time in the block for a number of years, have now been told that under the new categorization of "Aparthotel" they are only allowed to be resident for 9 months of the year – for the other 3 months, they must rent out their home. Nonsense? Of course it is, but it´s an ongoing battle at present. As always, though, well worth pointing out that this sort of thing is uncommon enough to be newsworthy.

Another example; Pedregeur (a very pleasant small town on the Costa Blanca North) has such major problems with feral cats and dogs that the Council has declared feeding of strays to be illegal. When that didn´t help the problem (mainly because nobody took any notice at all) they then decreed that the number of pets that individuals could keep in the town centre was to be restricted. Funnily enough, nobody has taken any notice of that, either, but there you go....

More widespread, and something you do need to check out, is the situation regarding **common features.** This arises if you are buying in, say, an apartment block with a communal pool and/or gardens. Many such developments will restrict you to the amount of animals you can have, and may insist that only dogs up to a certain weight are allowed. Also worth checking – particularly if you want to rent – is whether communal pools are open all year, or are restricted to just a few months in the summer.

Electricity consumption – Worth asking what the electricity rating for the property is. Iberdrola (the main electric company) band their charges according to consumption; the more you use, the higher the band. Fair enough, but the point is that if you use more than your banding allows, you will find your fuses suddenly trip when you have a number of appliances running at the same time. All villas under 10 years old will have a gadget fitted into the fuse box (looks like a large fuse, with blue writing on it) which stops this annoying tripping out. If your new box hasn't got one, get an electrician to fit it. Not just to stop the annoyance of having to re-set your fuses/switch appliances off; if you haven't got one, Iberdrola are entitled to start charging you at a higher band, whether you merit it or not.

Gas – Spain runs on gas bottles! Not the little, camping size ones you get in the UK, but big, heavy (17 kilos) bottles. There are 2 types; the flimsier, silver CEPSA bottles should only be for occasional use, for instance, for outdoor gas BBQ′s. The heavier orange REPSOL bottles are for use in the house, for your hob or gas fire, etc. Whichever one you use, you need to buy the first bottle, which is expensive as you then have it for life. You will need to give the vendor your name and address details and the all important NIE number, and actually sign an agreement for the bottle. After that, you just take the empty bottle to either a garage or garden centre (or REPSOL depot) and exchange it for a full one – at present, an exchange costs around €18. To give you an idea of usage; I have a gas hob in the kitchen, and I use it every day. A bottle lasts me around 9 months!

I have added the section on gas here both to let you know about buying the bottles, but also to explain about the certificates you need if you have "mobile" gas.

Firstly, if you have a gas bottle connection to the house, every 5 years REPSOL will knock on your door and ask to inspect your installation.

They will check that your gas pipes are in date (the pipe has an issue date on it) and may insist that it is replaced. They will also check the regulators and again, if they are faulty will replace them. They will charge you for this, and also for the certificate they issue to say everything is correct. Allow around €100 (+ iva) for the inspection and replacements. N.B. A favourite scam is to send out men with official looking clip boards, claiming to be from REPSOL. If your inspection isn't due, tell them to go away. If your inspection is due, ask to check their identification – it should be on official REPSOL letterhead, and they should also have picture ID. If you still don't like the look of them, ring your local Guardia – who will be with you in about 10 minutes. They will check back with REPSOL. If the Inspectors are genuine, they will not mind in the least – they're used to it. If they're bogus, they will fly as soon as you produce your mobile. This is also an extremely good chance to learn a few swear words in Spanish.

Secondly, if you have either a gas or oil central heating boiler, it is a legal requirement that it is serviced once a year, and that you have a certificate to say that it is in good working order. In practice, it's very common for the boiler to be serviced *san* certificate, which costs another €60.

Running Costs – It's quite reasonable to ask about household running costs – gas, electric, water/sewage and local taxes.

The are generally 2 local taxes which you should be aware of; IBI and "basura".

IBI is the main one. This is the equivalent of Council Tax in the UK, and is payable in autumn. It's based, according to a remarkably complex formula, on the rateable value of the property, which in itself is adjusted infrequently. It varies according to the size of the property, the size of the plot and the demands of the local council. To give you an idea, our IBI for a 3 bedroom villa with pool, on a 500sm plot, is currently €550 per year. The bigger your plot and house, the higher your IBI.

On the Costa Blanca, IBI (and other municipal taxes) are collected on behalf of the Council by an organization called "SUMA". Even very small towns will have a SUMA office, in the centre somewhere, or you can go on line at to their excellent website (and read it in English) at www.suma.es.

You may or may not have to pay Basura in addition to the IBI. "Basura" is the charge for rubbish disposal; some councils include it in the IBI payment; if you don´t have any rubbish bins or recycling facilities on or nearby your property, you shouldn't be charged Basura at all. It´s payable in the spring (I know, don´t ask me why it´s not autumn like the IBI, I have no idea). Our Basura is around €140 pa.

Assuming that you have mains water, it is metered, and payable to your local water company, generally every 3 months. Costs vary hugely depending on the source – if it´s desalinated sea water, it will be much more expensive than if it comes from a local aquifer.

And – very importantly – it´s not a tax, but if you are buying a property which has communal features – e.g. a communal swimming pool and/or gardens, or you are buying an apartment in a block – you will be charged annual maintenance costs. These should include upkeep of all outside areas, and things like painting and maintenance of the outside of the building. Charges vary hugely from place to place, and also depend on the features you are paying for, so make sure both that you know how much the communal charges will be, and also what they cover.

Remember, these do not replace IBI and basura; these are still payable in addition to your community fees.

Have there been any major insurance claims? – Well worth asking, and not just for the obvious reasons! In Valencia, if there is what is classified as a major disaster (flood, storms, abnormally high winds, etc) which causes widespread damage, 2 things happen. Firstly, the army and Guardia Civil move in quite remarkably quickly to give emergency aid. Secondly, the regional Government declares a state of emergency, and when this happens all insurance claims are met directly by the Valencian Government. You still claim via your insurers, but they immediately pass on the claim to Valencia and – amazingly – your no claims bonus is not affected as a result. But, equally interesting, if your vendor says Valencia has met a claim, then immediately ask for details. If there has been one flood, or mud slide, or demolished wall, there may well be another lurking for the next spell of abnormal weather!

The Neighbours! – No, I´m not being facetious. If you are intending to retire to the Costa Blanca, it´s a fair bet that you're looking forward to a bit of peace and quiet. If this is the case, ask if the surrounding properties are lived in full time, or whether they are rented out as holiday lets. If you have potential neighbours all around who let, then you are going to have very noisy summers, as holiday makers are not noted for their concern towards residents. If you don´t mind, fine. But if you do, well worth considering when you're making your choice of property. Also worth thinking about is proximity to local bars; lovely not to have to drive, of course, but will you still be happy at 1:00 in the morning, when the karaoke is going full swing?

Sounds like a long list, I know, but is it really that much longer than you would think about if you were buying in a strange town in the UK?

Chapter 5

"Land Grab"

Everybody assumes that this is a peculiarly Valencian problem, but it isn´t. A number of other provinces have also adopted Land Grab regulations, including Andalucia.

To get one common misconception out of the way first; Land Grab (or to give it it´s proper nomenclature, "Ley Reguladora de la Actividad Urbanistica (LRAU))" is **not** primarily aimed at ex-pats. It has also affected many Spaniards, and is enforced without regard to nationality.

It originally arose out of a piece of particularly bad legal drafting, which was aimed at utilizing areas which appeared – in the jargon of the legislation – "to be neglected or abandoned land". The LRAU was first enacted at the start of the construction boom in 1994, and some provincial local governments saw the law as a chance to use this hitherto useless land for building – originally, with the best of intentions, as it was hoped to use it for much-needed local housing and social projects. Alas, it didn´t take long for ruthless developers to see the potential loopholes in the law, and soon the system was becoming abused and was used to seize land from innocent property owners to develop new Urbanizations which did nothing to help social projects, but did create a vast amount of wealth for the developer, and, it must be said, the local authorities concerned.

So why does it concern us? Because LRAU has expanded way beyond the original, laudable intentions. This law allows unscrupulous developers to demand that land is reclassified from "rural" land (which cannot be built on) to "urbano" land without *seeking the owner's prior permission.* You may be surprised to learn that this is also allowed under UK law! Unfortunately, the LRAU has further implications. Not only can the developer have your lovely orchard reclassified without mentioning it to you, he can then go on to get a compulsory purchase order on the land after the reclassification has taken place, often, of course, at prices that are far below market value.

Even worse, unlike the UK scheme, you have no right of appeal. And even worse again, there have been cases where the property owner has not only been paid a pittance for their land, but has then been forced under the terms of the LRAU to **pay** the developer tens of thousands of euros to put the infrastructure in place for the new development that is built on his former land! To add insult to injury, LRAU requires only 15 working days notice to be given to property owners, to enable them to present an objection, or alternative schemes. Even if you are actually in Spain, this is, of course, nowhere enough time, particularly as it will probably take you longer than 15 days to get over the shock.

There have, of course, been tremendous backlashes to the inequity of the scheme, and as a result, changes have been made. In 2004, Valencia promised reform to the law and to bolster the legal position of small landowners. The LRAU law was amended in 2006 with LUV (Ley Urbanistica Valencia). Unfortunately, this actually changed very little as it did not address key issues and still left land owners open to abuse from unscrupulous developers.

Other areas of Spain have implemented different versions of LRAU which in some cases are just as onerous, if not more so, but for some reason are far less publicisized. In any event, worth noting that Valencian LRAU only applies to the provinces of Alicante, Valencia and Castellon, but unfortunately definitely applies to the whole of the Costa Blanca area.

So, what can you do to protect yourself from this most iniquitous of laws? If you're buying on an established Urbanization, you're virtually safe. If you're buying a plot, particularly a large one, check first that the **whole of the plot is classified as "urbano" already.**

Problems may arise if you fall in love with a rural house, on a big plot. Before you put down a euro in deposit, talk to your Abogado. If the whole plot is rated "urbano", there should be no problem. If part or all of it is classified as "rural" or "non urbano", think twice! Your Abogado may be able to get it reclassified, if not – look elsewhere as you are running the risk of your dream home turning into a nightmare.

To be honest, the LRAU isn't a threat to most of us, who choose to live on Urbanizations or in towns and villages. Even if you want a finca in the middle or nowhere, unless you have a huge garden, you will probably be safe, but make sure your Abogado checks for that all important "urbano" classification.

Since the construction market in Spain virtually collapsed a few years ago, LRAU has been less of a problem, simply because developers have been far more reluctant to build. But there are now signs that the housing market is picking up, and if the boom times return, then you can be sure that LRAU will become a problem again.

Even as I type, there are rumours circulating yet again that LRAU is to be de-legalized (and if it is, I do hope they get the drafting right this time) and that compensation will be paid to those who have suffered in the past. Lovely, but to be honest I will believe it when I see it. In the meantime, if you are buying on an urbanization, you should be safe. If you are buying in a rural area, if all of your land has been categorized "urbano" you should be safe. If you want a huge plot in the middle of nowhere with a wonderful view, and your Abogado tells you it is classified as "non urbano", don´t say you haven´t been warned!

Chapter 6

Forms, forms, forms….

Well, actually it´s not that bad. Most of them only have to be obtained once (at least under the current play of legislation) but getting them, if you don´t understand exactly what you need to do, can be a nightmare.

If you are going to be resident here in Spain, you need 3 forms to be completed – the "holy trinity". If you own property here but are not resident, then you will need a different set of forms. By "resident" I mean resident for tax purposes. And the definition of that is simple – you are resident for tax purposes if you live in Spain for more than 183 days per year. The British taxman treats the situation differently, talking in terms of "severing links" with the UK; whether you retain a property in the UK, how often you visit…. For purposes of living here on the Costa Blanca, take it as read that if you physically live here in Spain for more than 6 months of the year, the Hacienda will consider that you are a resident.

So, moving on to the basics. For Residents the forms you must have are:

NIE Number (which you already have)

Residencia Certificate

Padron *(certificate of empadronamiento))*

In addition to these "must have´s", once you are in residence, officially! – you may have to complete the dreaded Form 720. As this may not apply to everyone, I will deal with this at the end of the chapter. Again, I'm afraid its one of those forms that is far better dealt with by your Accountant, as it has to be completed and returned to the Hacienda within a fixed period, and there are fairly swinging penalties in place for getting it wrong, even if it´s entirely inadvertent.

Firstly, then, the **Residencia.** I should say at this point that I know quite a few English expats, who have lived here for years, who insist this business of obtaining a Residencia is totally unnecessary. They still pay tax in England, and if they need healthcare either pay privately on a "per visit" basis, or wait until they go back to England, where – of course! – they are still registered at their former local GP's practice. The fact that they are actually illegal immigrants seems to worry them not one bit …. It would me! Apart from that, there are huge advantages to being legally and **fiscally** resident if you actually live here. Your tax situation is far more favourable, you can access state health care, not worry 'too much about inheritance tax, buy a new (Spanish) car, access cheap holidays, join the local Pensionista club … and of course, you don't have to worry about the Guardia knocking on your door!

So, you've decided to get your Residencia Certificate, which proves that you are a resident foreign national. What do you need to do?

Before you actually apply, it's worth noting that obtaining a Residencia does not lose you a single one of your rights as a British Passport holder. You are still 100% a British citizen!

To obtain the Residencia, it means yet another trip to the same office where you obtained your NIE number. And again, you **must** make a prior appointment.

Your accountant or Abogado will have a number of appointment slips ready, or of course you can use one of the number of agencies who help us foreigners through this minefield. Costs will be around the €150 (+iva) mark. If you want to use an agent, ask them to help you fill in the relevant forms and also check that you have everything to hand before returning to make the actual submission. I found out the hard way that if it isn´t perfect, then you will get turned away.

If you would prefer to do it yourself, visit your Comisaria de Policia and say you wish to apply for a Residencia and want:-

1. A current list of the documents needed for making an application (they are available in several languages.)

2. An application form called Solicitud de Tarjeta en Regimen Comunitario (this is in triplicate.)

---

3. Form No.790

As usual, I'm afraid – unless you speak fluent Spanish – take an interpreter with you. At the same time as you pick up your forms, you can ask for an appointment time and date, but do leave yourself enough time to get the document pack together.

Take the Form 790 to your Spanish bank for completion. This form confirms your Spanish Bank account number and money held there (for this service you pay a very small fee.) If you are a Pensioner – either state or private - you must also ask the bank for a *Certificado Bancario* which confirms the amount of your pension and frequency of payment. You might get away with taking a hard copy of your bank statement (sorry, an online copy isn't sufficient), but I would advise going for the Certificado – all the banks are used to being asked for it, and it isn't a problem for them. You then return to the Police Station on the due date with:-

- **Completed Form 790** together with a photocopy

- **Certificado Bancario** together with a photocopy.

- **Medical Form S1** (which is the form from DWP in Newcastle that says you are no longer entitled to state health care in the UK) plus a photocopy, **or** your Spanish medical registration card (Tarjeta SIP), **or** if you are not entitled to a SIP card, evidence that you hold private medical insurance (usually a copy of your original contract with the health insurer) plus a photocopy, plus a photocopy of each side of the SIP card if you are using this as evidence of health entitlement.

- **Certifica de Empadronamiento (Padron)** plus a photocopy

- **Passport** and one photocopy

- **Four** passport size photographs.

Please ensure that you have a copy of everything – copying facilities are not available in the offices, and if you have to go away and get them, you will have to make another appointment and start all over again.

You can´t get a "family" Residencia, each individual has to get their own. The time scale for collecting them varies from office to office; it can be a couple of days, or – worse case – a couple of months. If you are using an agent, then they will be advised that the Certificate is ready, and can collect them for you. If you've been brave and done it all yourself, then you will be contacted directly (either by telephone or post) and told when the Certificate can be picked up. Once you have it, put it in the safe, or frame it – in any event, don't lose it! If you do, you will have to produce all the documents all over again – copies are not issued!

There is still some controversy over how long the Certificate actually lasts; there are rumblings that they will need to be renewed each 5 years, but as yet, nothing definite.

Sounds a lot of trouble for very little return? Well, as I said earlier it is a legal requirement that you are registered, if you live here for more than 183 days per year. It also means you pay less tax. If you own property in Spain, but are not registered as a resident, then the Hacienda immediately assumes that you are renting your property out, and imposes a tax called the "Renta". This is based on rateable value, in the same way as the IBI, and there is no arguing about it. If you own property and are not legally resident, then the Hacienda will demand Renta from you, and you **must** pay it even if you don't earn a penny in rental, and only ever use the property yourself.

Many people in the past got away without paying Renta. However, in recent years the Hacienda has realised what a huge, and entirely legal, revenue stream they have been ignoring, and they are now very keen not just to charge it, but also to pursue back tax that has not been paid. In addition to the Renta, if you are a non-resident property owner who **does** rent out their property, you are supposed to declare the gross amount of rental earned to the Hacienda, who then tax you 25% on that rental with no deductions for maintenance etc allowed. Strangely enough, not many people comply with this.

In addition to not paying Renta, being properly registered and **fiscally resident** (i.e. you pay income tax in Spain) has a huge impact on capital gains tax and inheritance tax liabilities – more on this aspect in the next chapter.

You will be relieved to know that obtaining the **Padron** is usually a much easier process. For this, you visit your local Town Hall (Ayuntamientio) – ask at the front desk where you need to go to get your Padron.

Again, ex-pats often seem to feel the Padron is voluntary. It is and it isn't! Whilst not a legal obligation, trying to live in Spain without a Padron is asking for problems.

Signing on to the Padron means you have registered with your Ayuntamiento as being a resident in their community; it means you have the right to vote in local and EU elections; you can enroll your children in local schools, and it is essential to obtain a SIP card for state healthcare. It also enables the Ayuntamiento to get money from central government to spend on behalf of the local community – the more residents on the Padron, the more money to spend on the community. And of course, no Padron, no Residencia!

To get your first Padron, take the following documents with you:

Passport (plus photocopy)
NIE Certificate (plus photocopy)
Deeds to your property ("Escritura") (plus photocopy) or rental contract of more than 6 months duration

And amazingly, normally you do not have to make an appointment, just turn up and join the queue (if any).

The Padron is rather an odd document in itself. Even though none of your personal circumstances have changed, your copy of the Padron is actually only valid for 3 months. Unless you need to actually produce the Padron, this isn't a problem, and in practice most people don't bother renewing it until they actually have to (for instance, if you want to change your car). When you do need to renew it, go back to your Ayuntament with:

The old Padron Certificate
Your passport
Your Residencia

It should then be no problem to be issued with a new certificate.

And penultimately in this section … the dreaded Form 720. At present, the Hacienda is emphasizing that submission of this form is for information only; they are not intending to attempt to tax anybody on the assets declared. For the future? Who knows ….

Before I get to the nitty gritty of Form 720, it is important to note that the €50,000 minimum referred to throughout is per person; unfortunately, this means that if you and your partner hold joint assets in joint names which are greater than €50,000 in total, then you both have to submit a Form 720. For example, my husband and I have the sterling equivalent of €50,000 in our joint bank account in England (I wish!). Even though this is a joint account, we cannot split and claim we own half each; as far as the Hacienda is concerned, we both must submit a Form 720

Basically, if you are an ex pat who is living permanently in Spain (i.e. you are fiscally resident) then you must submit a Form 720 if:

- You have money in offshore accounts (ie in banks which are not registerd in Spain) with a balance higher than €50,000. You have to give the Hacienda the full name and address of the bank or other financial institution, the account number or IBAN, the average amount in the account during the year, the amount at the end of the year, and if you are not the only owner, your percent of ownership.

- Other investments (shares, etc.) life or disability insurances with a value at cash in above €50,000 and annuities which are deposited, managed or obtained abroad, with a balance higher than €50,000 must also be declared.

- If you have real estate located located outside Spain with values higher than €50,000, this should be declared. You will need the full address of the property, the date of purchase or reception, its value at that time, and if you are not the full owner, your percent of ownership.

To put it at its simplest, if you – or you and your partner jointly - have assets worth more than €50,000 located outside Spain, then the Hacienda wants to know about it.

The only exception to this that I have been able to find is for certain tax-efficient offshore funds. If you have an offshore fund that enables you not to pay tax on the interest, (legally, that is!) then it may be exempt from the Form 720 requirements. I suggest you check with your Financial Advisor before you assume that yours is exempt; better safe than sorry!

Form 720 should be submitted between 1st January and 31st March. The only shred of good news is that, once submitted, you only have to submit another one if there is an increase of €20,000 in any one (or more) of the categories.

None of us likes it, but failure to file correctly can incur heavy monetary penalties, which are themsleves, in common with almost everything to do with the Hacienda, fairly complicated. In outline, the applicable penalties are:

- For not submitting the form at all, when you were liable to submit:

  Penalty: monetary fine of €5,000 for each item of information not included, with a minimum fine of €10,000.

- Submitting a form that is incomplete, inaccurate or with false information:

  Penalty: monetary fine of €5,000 for each item of information not included, inaccurate or false, with a minimum fine of €10,000.

- Submitting the form outside of the legal term, but before the request of the Spanish tax authorities to submit it:

  Penalty: monetary fine of €100 for each item of information in each category, with a minimum fine of €1,500.

- Not submitting the form electronically:

  Penalty: monetary fine of €100 for each item of information in each category, with a minimum fine of €1,500.

And finally… as from 2014 (retrospective for the 2013 tax year), it has become necessary to submit a Wealth Tax Declaration, in addition to Form 720 and Income Tax declaration.

This declaration is only required if your WORLDWIDE assets owned are over €700.000 net per person. And unfortunately, this includes both assets owned in Spain as well as anywhere else in the world. It includes any property that you own in Spain, even if it is the property where you live.

The slightly good news is that the value of any property outside Spain can be reduced by the amount of mortgage remaining to be repaid on the property. This reduction also applies to your Spanish property.

In addition, the first €300.000 of your main Spanish property is exempt from payment of the tax.

If you are still lucky enough to own net assets with a value of more than €700.000 per person, then you will have to submit the Wealth Tax Declaration.

At the moment, there is no information available on how much the rate of tax is, nor what the penalties are for not submitting, or submitting incorrectly. Nor is there any clarification on how all this is effected by the double-taxation treaty that Spain has in place with the UK.

Yet another case, I'm afraid, of needing to have a chat with your Accountant. Hopefully, this area will become much clearer in the next couple of years.

Chapter 7

Taxes in Spain

As the saying goes; "There are only 2 certainties in life; taxes and death." But it´s not all bad in Spain!

Starting with **Income Tax.** If you are resident in Spain, then you should make an income tax return to the Hacienda every year. **You should do this even if you have no income to declare, or even if it is below the taxable limit.** and you must ensure that both you and your partner are registered for tax. ¥

Firstly the bare bones of how to make a declaration.

Unlike the UK, if you are living in Spain and are not employed "on the books", (for instance, if your sole income is from pensions) then you make one tax declaration every year. This is retrospective for the last tax year; must be submitted between 1st March and 20th June, and now has to be in electronic format.

As in the UK, you receive a tax-free allowance (somewhat more advantageous if you are a couple); this increases at age 65, and again at age 70. There are also allowances for children still living with you at home, or for elderly dependants who live with you. Amazingly – as you have never paid into the Spanish Social Security system – if you "earn" less than your total tax-free allowance, you will receive a tax rebate!

Any income that is not taxed elsewhere (see below) including UK pensions and income from annuities must be declared. Spain has a double taxation agreement with the UK, so you will not be taxed in the UK as well (providing, of course, that you have dealt with the UK taxman before you left, and explained to him that you will be paying tax in Spain. As soon as you get your Residencia, contact him again and tell him once more!)

Before you leave the UK permanently, apply for Certificate E101 from the tax authorities. For more information on double taxation between the UK and Spain, go to http://www.hmrc.gov.uk/cnr/dtdigest.pdf). There is a slender chance that you may end up paying tax in the UK and Spain for the first year, but you will get this refunded by the UK. This appears to happen occasionally as a result of administration problems in the UK, but it is far, far rarer than those people who are still doggedly paying tax in the UK claim.

You can make the submission to Hacienda yourself, but I don't anybody who is brave enough. The form is long, complicated, and not only in Spanish, but in "legal" Spanish. Make life easy and let your Accountant do it for you, is my advice. If you do this, you will need to give your Accountant the following documents, each year:

If you are a UK state pensioner:

- DWP letter re. State Pension for the current and last tax year, together with - if you are in receipt of any private (company) pensions, the relevant P60 (s) for the current and last tax year

If you receive only company pension(s), then you must submit the relevant P60's.

- If applicable, annuity certificate(s) and policy(s) showing commencement of pension

In all cases, you must also submit:

- Statements from UK banks showing interest received and tax retentions (If you don´t get these automatically, contact your bank and ask for one)

- Statements from Spanish banks showing interest received and tax retentions (These tend to arrive without question, but if you only get online statements etc, it´s very easy to print one off from your statement page – look for the heading "Tax Information".)

- Certificates of dividends received with Tax Credits (UK and Spain)

If you have sold or purchased a property during the relevant tax year, you must also submit:

- Escritura (Deeds) of Purchase AND Escritura of Sale of all property concerned

- Receipts for construction work etc. undertaken on the property sold. §

You will also need to submit your Residencia Certificate(s) and a copy of last year's income tax declaration after the first declaration.

I know, it sounds horrifically complicated, but after the first year it doesn't take more than a few minutes to complete. Make sure you keep all your relevant documents filed together from year to year, and it's easy.

And one final word on income tax in Spain, and definitely an item that you may find advantageous. For some odd reason, *civil service pensions are not taxable in Spain.* In practice, this means that if you are in receipt of any form of public service pension from the UK, then it is still taxed in the UK, not Spain. For all practical reasons, as long as your Civil Service pension **is** taxed in the UK, then the Hacienda simply does not want to know about it – you do not need to submit it in any shape or form in Spain. This is extremely advantageous, not just from the point of view of cutting down on the paperwork – always a blessing! – but also because it means that effectively you have 2 tax allowances – your Spanish allowance for all income that is taxable in Spain, and your full English tax allowance for your civil service pension. Again, this is something you need to talk to the UK taxman, and your pension provider, about before you leave the UK, but it shouldn't be complicated for you as the Overseas Branch of the Tax Office in the UK is used to dealing with this situation. Nor does it mean that you have to have your Civil Service pension paid into a UK bank, it can still come over to Spain if you prefer.

If you own more than one property in Spain (or if you are not a Spanish Resident your main residence is liable) then you will be liable for the **Renta** on each property that is not your main residence. Remember, you should also declare all your rental income on any property you own, including your main residence (not as odd as it sounds; I know a number of ex-pats who make a nice little bit on the side by converting their underbuilds to a self-contained apartment, and renting it off in the summer.).

Moving on to **Capital Gains Tax (CGT)** in Spain. Again, unfortunately the situation is completely different to the UK, and it´s an area many ex-pats find confusing, not least because it´s not something you have to deal with regularly.   Even native born Spaniards often find it difficult!

CGT is payable on the profits you make when you sell your property in Spain. "Profit" in this case is the excess difference between your original purchase price (as stated on your Escritura) and the sale price, with buying and selling costs (tax and legal fees) deducted.

If you are **fiscally resident in Spain** (i.e. you have made an income tax submission to the Hacienda **for at least the past 5 years**) the CGT rate is **15%.** If you are not fiscally resident, a flat rate of **35%** is applied. Good enough reason for completing your tax return to the Hacienda???? If you purchase a property from a non-resident, you are required to withhold 5% of the total purchase price and pay it directly to the tax authorities – this is another reason why your Accountant wants to know if you have bought or sold property in the tax year.

There are some advantageous exceptions to the basic figures. These are:

- If you are a fiscal resident aged over 65, and are selling your principal Spanish residence where you have lived for over 3 years, you are exempt from CGT entirely.

- If you are a fiscal resident aged over 65 and have taken advantage of one of the "lifetime mortgage" schemes, where essentially you sell all or part-interest in your property, but retain the right to sell it, or live in it until your death, you are exempt from CGT.

- If you are a fiscal resident who invests **all** of the sale proceeds of your principal residence to purchase another principal residence, you are CGT exempt, providing you have lived in the sold property for more than 3 years. If you only use part of the property sale price to buy another principal residence, you get a percentage relief known as "rollover credit". In practice, it works like this:

You paid €120,000 for your house, and sold it for €180,000, giving you a gross profit of €60,000. You buy a new house as your main residence, which costs you €180,000. In this case, you have invested all returns for your original property, and there is no CGT payable.

If, however, your new house costs only €90,000, then you will have to pay CGT on €30,000, because half of your "profit" has been reinvested in the new house.

- When you are doing your calculations for CGT purposes, don´t forget to produce all receipts for construction work on the property, as these are deducted from your liability for CGT.

-    All official expenses in acquiring a property can be used to offset against CGT - taxes and fees, i.e., transfer tax for resale property or IVA for new property, expenses for the notary, property registration, the "plus valia" tax (see below) and Abogado´s fees. You must have the official receipts to be able to claim them.

If you own more than one property in Spain, and are selling a property that is not your main residence, then CGT will be calculated in the same basic way as for a main residence, but unfortunately with none of the exemptions (except for selling and buying costs). You may be able to claim an inflation-linked allowance, based on how long you have owned the property. It may also be advantageous to talk to your Financial Expert about putting all your property into an English limited company, but I´m afraid all of this area is way outside the scope of this guide. If this applies to you, talk to the experts in this area!

Another really heavyweight "nasty" in the Spanish tax area is **Inheritance Tax.** And again, it really is advantageous to be fiscally resident in this respect, and it is highly recommended that you – and your partner – draw up Spanish wills as soon as possible. Without them, life can get very complicated just at the exact time when you really want things to be as simple as possible. Most people have "mirror wills" that simply give each partner the same rights in case of the death of the other partner. If you still have assets in England, ensure you also have English wills to take care of this.

Before I dive in to the intricacies of Spanish Inheritance tax, a word about a very basic and very important aspect of it. Inheritance Tax arises if you inherit something, **even if you have no intention of selling it.** This is particularly important between spouses; if you own assets (including your only Spanish residence) jointly, then when one of you dies the other is liable for Inheritance Tax on the half that they have inherited, no matter that they fully intend to carry on living there!

Very basically, Spanish Inheritance Tax works like this:

- If you are an ex-pat fiscally resident in Spain, then you are liable to pay Spanish Inheritance Tax **regardless of where the inheritance is actually situated** (i.e. you will be taxed on an inheritance in the UK, or anywhere else in the world). Fortunately, as a result of the double-taxation treaty with the UK, you will only be liable for tax in Spain, and not also in the UK. Even more fortunately, **if your legatees are resident in Valencia,** they receive massive tax advantages. If you are non-resident, then you are liable to pay Inheritance Tax only on assets actually located in Spain.

- There are 4 classes of "inheritors" with different allowances for each class. The figures given in brackets are the relevant allowances, correct as at 2014. These classes are:

- Group 1: "Natural descendants" (children) and adopted children under age 21. (15,956.87€).

- Group 2: Natural descendants and adopted children over 21, spouses, parents and adoptive parents (15,956.87€).

- Group 3: Brothers/sisters, nephews/nieces, aunts/uncles (7,993.46€).

- Group 4: Relatives in forth degree or friends (what are known in Spain as "non-blood"). (No allowances).

The reason for distinguishing between **Groups 1 and 2** is that there is a graduated threshold for **Spanish inheritance tax payments** for children and grandchildren under the age of 21. For every year that **each** child is under the age of 21 they receive an additional **€3,990 for non-residents and €8,000 for residents** up to a maximum allowance of **€47,858/ 96,000€ respectively**.

It is also worth noting that non-married partners who are part of a legal, civil partnership, are only classed as Group 4 for Inheritance Tax purposes. Even more strangely, if you live in Murcia, a non-married partner is classed as a spouse. Unfortunately, this is not the case on the Costa Blanca, where you would be relegated to a Group 4, no matter how long you had been together.

And apologies yet again for banging on about the importance of being fiscally resident; the following table gives the general, Spain wide, allowances you are entitled to before Inheritance Tax is charged. Look at the differences between Resident's allowances (Column 1) and Non-Resident's allowances (Column 2)! In addition, **check out the paragraph following the Chart regarding special (and extremely advantageous) tax exemptions for Valencian residents.**

Also worth bearing in mind is the timescale for submission of Inheritance Tax demands. You have **6 months** in which to pay your tax. After this, it´s a fine for late payment of 5% for every 3 months overdue, up to a maximum of 20% extra.

The rate at which Inheritance Tax is payable varies on a sliding scale from 7.65% to a massive 34%, depending on the value of the assets.

All figures are accurate as at 2014.

Group	Resident	Non-resident
1. Descendent below the age of 21 (includes children and grandchildren)	€40,000 for each child with an additional €8,000 for every year they are under 21 to a maximum of **€96,000**	€15,956.87 for each child with an additional €8,000 for every year they are under 21 to a maximum of **€47,858**
2. Grandchildren and children older than 21, parents, spouse	€40,000 each beneficiary	€15,956 each beneficiary
3. Sisters, brothers, aunts/ uncles, nephews/ nieces and parents in law	€7,993 each	€7,993 each
4. Others (not "blood" relation	No allowance applies	No allowance applies

As if all that wasn't complex enough, as this is Spain we're talking about, the Inheritance Tax rules and regulations vary from province to province. Fortunately for those of who live on the Costa Blanca, **and are fiscally resident** in Valencia, under Valencian tax laws, there is a ray of light for us. **There are special Tax deductions in the Valencia region for surviving spouses who are themselves resident in Valencia.** Roughly translated from the legalese, this means that both you and your husband or wife must be have lived in Valencia, and both have been registered to pay tax here, for a 5 year period before the taxable event happened.

Basically, in addition to the allowances set out above, for the *resident surviving spouse*, **the allowance against Inheritance Tax is €100,000, and a further discount of 75% is allowed on the actual tax payable**. However, this only refers to **resident heirs**

Obviously, this is a very complex and very expert field, and I have done no more than scratch the surface here, to give you an idea of what to expect. To get a definitive picture of your own case, I urge you strongly to speak to your Financial Expert or Abogado, preferably before the issue arrises! Don't just use this as the definitive answer to all things Inheritance Tax; it isn't, and I am not a

Spanish lawyer. This area is intended to give you an outline of the Spanish tax situation, and no more. Basically, it's only meant to let you know how complex the issue is, and to raise your awareness of the issues involved. Each individual case is different, and you **must** consult your own legal representative to get a definitive answer regarding your own liability.

Before I leave the vexed question of Inheritance Tax, it's worthwhile to take a look at (legal) ways to minimise the problem.

- You might want to consider buying in the joint names of future inheritors, or even selling, fully or in part to those inheritors. Obviously, this is an area that requires not only careful consideration, but a lot of legal advice as well.

- If you can bear to do it, take out a mortgage on the property. Any amount owing on the mortgage is deducted before working out your Inheritance Tax.

- Either buying via, or transferring the property to, an EU or English limited company. This will incur set up and annual maintenance fees, but could be well worth while, particularly if the amount of beneficiaries is limited and you only have, say, a single spouse's allowance of €40,000 for all your assets.

After the intricacies of Inheritance Tax, the **PLUS VALIA** almost comes as a light relief. Almost ....

You may remember I referred to this pages ago, in the introduction. I promised you more, and here it is!

Basically, the Plus Valia is a local capital gains tax, set by your local Ayuntamiento. It´s based on the increase of the value of the land your property is built on, from the date you bought it, to the date you are selling or inheriting it. The value will vary according to the area the land is located in, with rural land being charged at a lower rate than, say, an urbanisation.

Normally, the Seller pays this Plus Valia, unless you come to an agreement with your purchaser that he pays for it. The tax is calculated according to the rateable value of the property, and the number of years you have owned it.

To pay this tax, you need to take along a copy of the

new deed (copia simple) obtained from the Notary when the transaction is carried out to your local SUMA office who will then process a paying in slip for you and the payment can be made over the counter at most banks.

You can ask at SUMA or the town hall for an estimate of the Plus Valía before the signing at the Notary.

You will be forgiven at this stage for thinking, "Good heavens, a straightforward Spanish tax!" Alas, this is not always the case…

In recent years, property prices have fallen dramatically on the Costa Blanca (although they are now on the rise again) and some vendors have even taken a loss on property when selling it. Because of this, and the former common practice of "black money", some Ayuntiamentos have imposed what is best described as an "under the counter" Plus Valia.

It works like this. You fall in love with a villa and argue the price down dramatically. Fine. You have agreed that your Vendor will pay the Plus Valia, so as far as you are concerned, this is not an issue. But it could be! Up to a couple of years after legal completion of your bargain purchase, you could get a Plus Valia demand from the Ayuntamiento, and they expect **you** to pay it, not your Vendor. Why? Because the Ayuntamiento has decided that you have paid less than the market value for your villa, and as a result, they are going to tax you on the difference between what you paid, and what they consider the market value actually is. This practice has, supposedly, been outlawed but it´s worth bearing it in mind in case your bargain goes sour.

And that, I am pleased to say, is that as far as taxes are concerned. Unless, of course, the powers that be decide to dream up some new ones ....

¥ The reason for this is, if you are "fiscally resident" – and you can only be fiscally resident if you make a tax submission each year – then you will qualify for preferential treatment in capital gains tax, and inheritance tax. If you are not fiscally resident, the tax implications can be punitive. You DO NOT need to actually pay income tax to be fiscally resident, just make the annual return every year.

§   It's vital that you keep all receipts for construction work, no matter how small. If you sell your property at a profit from your original purchase price, you may be liable for Capital Gains Tax on the difference. Every euro spent on construction work can be deducted from your "profit", so hang on to them.

Chapter 8

Healthcare on the Costa Blanca

Before I plunge into the intricacies of healthcare on the Costa Blanca, I should make it clear at this point that I am assuming that you have been sensible, and got your Residencia. If you haven´t, then sorry – your choice is limited to paying for private health care. You cannot access state healthcare, full stop.

Firstly – and well worth saying – state healthcare in Spain is excellent. The NHS in the UK is graded Number 18 in the world; Spain is Number 7. Generally, waiting lists for hospital treatment are shorter than they are in the UK, and getting an appointment with your GP is rarely a problem. Unless you live in one of the main towns, or speak fluent Spanish, you will probably have to take an interpreter with you, but that's a small drawback. You generally need an interpreter even if your doctor speaks some English (and most do) to protect both you and your doctor – your health is a serious matter, and the medical staff want to be sure they understand exactly what your problem is. Look at it this way; in Spanish "knee" is "rodilla". "Rodillo" is a paint roller …. See what I mean?

It's well worth bearing in mind that it is likely to be a while before you will be fully on the system, so bring a good stock of any prescription medicine with you, from the UK. You can get most medicines (even those that are only available on prescription in the UK) from the pharmacy without a prescription here, but it can be costly. Also remember to bring a copy of each prescription you have – these will be needed by your new doctor, once you get on the system.

Moving on to what you are entitled to. The division here is based on whether you have a UK **state pension**, or if you are not old enough to receive one, i.e. you are "an under age ex-pat." In either case, congratulations on choosing to live on the Costa Blanca! Valencia is far more generous in terms of ex-pat healthcare than many other Spanish provinces, mainly because so many of us ex-pats have the sense to choose to live here.

The easy part is if you are in receipt of a **UK State pension**. If this is the case, you are entitled to receive full state healthcare in the Costa Blanca, on exactly the same basis as a Spaniard. And it's also quite easy to get on the system, once you know what to do.

Before you leave the UK, contact the DWP (formerly the DHSS) at Newcastle (telephone 01912187777) and ask them for a S1 form (previously Form E121). As this can take a couple of weeks to come through, I suggest doing it in good time before you leave the UK. When you arrive in Spain, and have all your other documentation sorted out, make an appointment at your local INSS office (Spanish Social Security). The website (http://www.seg-social.es/) – which is in English as well as Spanish – is very helpful and gives all the addresses, telephone numbers and locations of the INSS offices nationwide. As always, you **must** make a prior appointment, but you can either ring your local office for this, or do it on line via the website.

The official line from DWP is that you only need your Form S1 to get on the system. Personally, I don´t believe a word of it, and I would strongly advise taking your Residencia, Padron and Passport (plus, as always, copies of each document) with you as well. If you need healthcare before you get your SIP card, you should be able to use your English EHIC card in an emergency. If you´re really desperate, try signing on with just the S1, it may work! As always, take an intepreter with you.

You will have to fill in a form at the INSS offices. Once this is done, they should stamp your form, and give you a copy. You then take this to Reception at your local health centre, together with – you guessed it! – your Padron, Residencia and passport. I know, you've already produced these yesterday at the INSS offices, but why bother kicking agaisnt the inevitable? Much easier and quicker to produce them yet again.

The Health Centre will process your documents while you wait, and you will then be given a SIP card (Tarjeta de Sanitoria). Often, the first one has an expiry date of 3 months, to allow all your paperwork to be processed. In the week prior to expiry, take it back to your Health Centre and ask at Reception for a permanent card. Once you get your SIP card, guard it with your life and take a copy of it, just in case you do lose it! If you do have the misfortune to misplace it, take your photocopy back to the Health Centre and ask for a replacement.

When you get your SIP card, it will have the name of your new doctor on the reverse. If you need to make an appointment, you can either ring the Health Centre, queue at the Recption Desk, or go on line (dead easy, click on http://www.san.gva.es/ and look for "Cita Privia" – it's in

Spanish, but it´s illustrated and very simple to follow). Whichever method you use, you´ll need your SIP card handy.

A quick word regarding the EHIC card. In the past, ex-pats who were either not registered in Spain, or who couldn´t be bothered to get a SIP card, used these to try amd get routine health care. The UK Goverrnment has now got very annoyed about this, and are insisting that they should only be used for real emergencies, AND are not to be used at all in Spain if you are resident here Bottom line; if you are resident, either get a SIP card, or private health insurance. Health Centres and hospitals in Spain are following the UK lead, and are clamping down on "health tourism" generally. You may well find that if you try and use an EHIC for anything less than an emergency, and if you are resident even then, you will be charged. Don´t say you haven´t been warned!

OK, like us, you are a **non-state pension age ex-pat** wanting to move to the Costa Blanca permanently. In this case, you have 2 choices open to you. You can either **pay €60 per month to the Valencian Health Care Authorities**, which allows you to access the state healthcare system, or you can take out **private health**

insurance. Or both, of course, if you want. Eithe way, the good news is that you will not be left without healthcare.

You may have read that "young" (and isn´t it nice to be too young for *something!)* ex-pats can still access the state healthcare system in Valencia, without cost. This is an unfortunate half-truth, and if you are considering moving now, or in the near future, unfortunately you have missed the boat. There was an initiative last year (2013) between the UK Governemtn and Valencia which enabled younger ex-pats to obtain state health care, but it was only open for a limited period, and depended upon you having been resident here since 2012.

The only way you can now access state healtchare (and this will entitle you to state healthcare Spain-wide, not just in Valencia) is to contribute €60 per month to the "Convenio Especial." This is administered by the Regional Health Authorty in Valencia. For your €60, you will get **full** state healthcare, which will cover all normal healthcare services from GP to hospitalization. It also includes full cover for **pre-existing conditions, at no extra cost.** What it doesn´t cover is reduced cost prescriptions; you have to pay full price for all these, and some mdeication is very expensive. To give you an example, my husband is an insulin-dependant diabetic, who takes 2 types of insulin per day. His monthly bill for full priced insulin would be €120.

In order to access the shceme, you need to complete a form (now there´s a surprise) and submit it to the Valencian Healthcare Authority. You **must** have been registered on the Padron for **at least 1 year prior to your application**, presumably to ensure that you are actually resident, and not just a "health tourist". The instructions for applying are as follows:

- Download the relevant form from the website **here** under "Impresos asociados".

- Once the form is completed, you will also need a copy of your NIE form; a copy of your passport and a copy of an up to date pardon.

- Send everything to :

    Registro de la Dirección Territorial de Sanidad – Valencia
    Gran Vía Fernando El Católico, 74 46008 Valencia

I´m afraid that once they have processed your application, you will have to attend the offices in Valencia **in person** to sign your documents. I´ve checked with both Valencia and the UK Foreign Office about this, and although both have been supremely helpful, it appears that there´s no way around it – you have to sign in person.

Once you have been accepted, hot foot it to your local Health Centre with your papers from Valencia, padron and Reisdencia and pasport, and you will be issued with a SIP card.

If you prefer to go private, you have a wide choice. Many of the big UK private health providers (BUPA, etc) also provide cover in Spain. If you have an existing policy, it should be easy to bring it with you. If you would prefer a purely Spanish company, here are a few to go at (in no particular order):

ASSA
Direct Seguros (seguros is the Spanish word for insurance)
Zurich   Insurance
Allianz   Insurance
Liberty   Seguros
Axa

DKV	
Aegon	
Asefa	Seguros
Aviva	
Adeslas	
Assisa	
Sanitas	
Generali	Seguros
Groupama	

And many more! These are all national companies, but there is also a purely Valencian company called "Perpetuo Socorro". Hands up, we have used Perpetuo since we arrived, and 2 cataract operations, 2 knee replacements, an emergency gall bladder removal and an hernia repair later they are still providing me with excellent service, so I am a trifle biased in their favour. And this is definitely the one and only piece of advertising I am making!

Companies base your premiums on either your age (in which case cover costs more annually) or the amount you use the service. Some exclude pre-existing conditions, other offer limited cover (for instance, out patient cover may be included, but not hospital treatment).

There are a number of agencies who will be happy to get quotes for you – just check the weekly papers or go online.

As with the "pay as you go" national healhcare scheme, **any prescriptions issued by your private health doctor must be paid for at full price**.

Whichever scheme you go for, don't forget that once you – or your partner . get to UK state pension age, you should immeidately ask for a Form S1, and sign on to the Spanish national health for free. As soon as you get your free SIP card, if you are on the €60 per month scheme, write to Valencia (same address as you sent your original forms) and explain why you are resigning from the paid scheme.

And finally in this section – prescriptions. The method of obtaining prescriptions ("recetas" in Spanish) has changed at least 4 times in the 8 years we have lived here. Currently, you see your doctor at least once per year (as distinct from seeing him or her for medical attention) to get a review of your medications. At this review, he will update your needs on the computer, and issue you with a sheet (or more, depending on how much medication you have) setting out your drug useage. There will also be another sheet giving the dates you need to visit the pharmacy. This sheet **is vital.** At present, if you have more than one prescription item you visit the pharmacy every 2 weeks, and on each visit you will receive a portion of your prescription needs for the month. If you have only one item, you go once a month. It´s supposed to cut down on hoarding, but I have my doubts! At the pharmacy (and I strongly advise using the same one – they will have you on their computer, and will reserve items for you) hand over your "calendar" and your SIP card. If you are of pension age, you will pay a portion of the cost – currently no more than 10% of costs, up to a ceiling of €8 per month.

If you have to buy an expensive medical item from the pharmacy for which you don't have a prescription, keep the box and the receipt. Take them down to your Health Centre; the process varies from place to place, but you can either obtain a state prescription at Reception, or make an appointmetn with your doctor and ask him for a prescription for the item. Take the box, your SIP card and the prescription back to the pharmacy and they will give you a refund for most of the cost.

Bad news if you have a chronic condition, which would mean you are exempt from all prescription costs in the UK. This doesn't happen in Spain – as a pensioner, you will still have to pay your 10% or €8 per month.

And even worse news if you are an insulin dependant diabetic. Unlike the UK, in Spain you get only 1 prescription **per year** for testing strips, and all needles have to be bought. Needles cost around €16 - €18 per box of 100 (depending on length). Testing strips are expensive – I generally buy a job lot on e-bay and my husband still uses his old UK testing machine.

There are rumours that the prescription service is going to become fully electronic, which would be excellent, but I'm not holding my breath.

Chapter 9

Police in Spain

You will be forgiven for wondering why on earth I have included a whole chapter on policing in Spain. The reason is simple; unlike the UK, where you may spend entire decades without coming into contact with the police service at all, in Spain you **will** visit the police in some shape or form, and not only that, there are a lot of divisions between the different branches of the police. You need an offical form? Guardia Civil! You´ve had a minor traffic accident? Policia Local! You´ve been burgled? Policia National! You want to report noisy neighbours? Policia Local! You want to pay a traffic fine .... Actually, it´s the Correos (post office) for that!

So here goes! All of the following information has been kindly supplied by our local Guardia Civil representative, which is as good an indication as any as to the excellent service the Spanish police provide.

There are basically 3 divisions of the police force in Spain; Guardia Civil; Local Police and National Police.

Firstly, the **Guardia Civil.** These are the chaps you are going to come across most. Not only do they supervise areas like obtaining your NIE number and Resdiencia, they are also the traffic division ("Trafico") who deal with all things transport related outside of towns. These are the guys who will stop you if you are speeding or forget to switch your lights on if you go through a road tunnel. They have fairly wide ranging powers, and can stop cars "on demand" if they are at all supsicious. Quite often, they simply stop a certain amount of cars, just to make a document check. (Or possibly all blue cars; or all cars over a certain age; or all cars that need a good wash – I´ve never been able to work out what the actual criteria are). I was once stopped by a very nice young Guardia officer early on a Saturday morning when I was on my way for voluntary work at the local Cat Sanctuary; he was going to ask me to blow into the breahtalyzer until he found 4 middle aged ladies, dressed to clean, all beaming at him. For some reason, he decided not to bother ..... More seriously, Trafico are empowered to make on the spot fines, for areas like speeding, using a mobile fine whilst driving, not having a valid MOT, failing to stop at a stop sign, etc.

Confusingly, Guardia Civil also undertake "normal" police duties and can often be found patrolling towns and urbanisations in a deterrent role.

In additon, the Guardia Civil are also responsible for fighting smuggling; illegal weapons and explosives; control of border points (ports and airports); transfer of convicts and detainees; and control of nature and environmental regulations.

You may think there´s not a lot left for the other 2 groups, but they also have their own distinct functions. The **Policia Local** have a presence in virtually all towns, no matter how small. They are the equivalent of the local police force in England, and in practice share some duties with the Guardia Civil.

According to our local Guardia Officer, Fran, the main function of the Local Police is "to provide assistance in cases of emergency, catastrophe or calamity"! By which I think he means they are the first line of contact for any domestic emergency such as burglaries, assualt, etc.

The Policia Local are also the guardians of the town – one of their official tasks is to protect the local authorities and official buildings, and to guard public places during demonstrations or marches. The Spanish are not at all shy about making their feelings known if they do not like political activites, and demonstrations – which tend to be extremely noisy – are far from rare. On the lighter side, the Policia Local also mainain law and order during the numerous fiestas we all enjoy. The Policia Local will also try and mediate in domestic conflicts, whether summoned by the participants or the neighbours when they think things have gone on long enough.

The Policia Local, rather than the Guardia, also deals with traffic accidents within the town where they are based; if there is an accident on the highway outside the town, then this is looked after by Tráfico.

Policia Local are also "the eyes and ears of the Town Hall"; they deal with areas such as problem dogs; noise pollution, illegal constructions; traffic lights; and generals supervision of traffic in town. If you get a parking ticket in your local town, it will be placed on your windscreen by the Policia Local, not Tráfico.

As you would expect, the National Police deal with more serious crimes. They enforce and prosecute drug related crime; co-operate with international police forces; etc. Having said that, if you have a police related problem (for instance, you have been burgled) it is absolutely fine to ring the National Police, rather than your local Policia. The National Police may well pass your call on to the local chaps, **but** it´s worth noting that the National Police will **always** have facilities to respond to your initial call in English, whereas there is no guarantee that your local police station will have a resident English speaker. The emergency number in Spain for Fire, Ambulance and Police is **112.**

You may also be unfortunate enough to get caught up in a road "purge" undertaken by the National Police. No mistaking it if you come across it, the road will be coned off and there will be a number of very serious looking policemen standing around, normally clutching machine guns. These usually happen when the police have a tip off about drug shipments or (increasingly often, I´m afraid) illegal immigrants in transit. If they ask you to stop, then do so, don´t bother protesting your innocence, it will only take longer. If you are stopped, you will be asked to produce all your documentation and the police will probably make a very thorough search of your vehicle. If they find your documentation isn´t in order, it will be passed on to Tráfico, and you will eventually get a letter from them.

Don´t worry, without fail, all the Spanish police I have come across, no matter which division they come from, are unfailingly polite and courteous. They **all** carry guns, but I have yet to see one drawn in anger. And – amazingly – if they get it wrong, they will apologise. I once had a parking fine which got very, very complicated as for some reason it wasn't my registration number on the paperwork. Our lovely Fran sorted it out for me, and I even got a letter of apology from the Guardia Civil Sergeant.

Still had to pay the fine, though.

Chapter 10

Driving in Spain

I really don´t want to upset you, but driving in Spain is **complicated.** It´s not just a matter of driving on the "wrong" side of the road, and going around roundabouts the wrong way, sorry! It´s even more complicated than getting all your forms in order. You can, of course, take the easy route and simply refuse to abide by any of the rules and regulations, but if you get stopped for a document check, you **will** get a fine. And Tráfico will follow up on it, to make sure you have got it right. And even worse, if you have a traffic accident, you may find that your insurance company refuses to pay up, if your documentation is seriously awry.

The good news is that, if you do it right and take it step by step, it all breaks down nicely and even begins to look quite sensible, when you´ve lived here for a while.

The easy route first – you want to buy a new, Spanish registered car, or a second-hand Spanish car from a dealer. (The "from a dealer" aspect for a second-hand car is important – I´ll explain why later).

First, get all your documentation in order. *Officially*, to buy a new or second-hand vehicle you will need the full set of: Residencia, Padron, NIE number and passport. However, we bought our first Spanish new car from Opel without Padron or Residencia. I´m not sure how the dealer got around the legalities, but he did, and we never had any problems. Our second car got the full suite of documents, but again – no problems. The cost of a new car in Spain is now comparable to that in Britain, but be warned trade-in prices are considerably lower (garages take the official book price, and that is what you get). On the other hand, second-hand cars sold through a dealer tend to be quite expensive.

You do pay **road tax** (I know, there is no tax disc, but you still pay it!) and it´s based on emissions, as in the UK. Oddly, road tax varies considerably from town to town, as it´s set by the Ayuntamiento wherever you buy the car from. You also need **car insurance** (generally, I have found this to be cheaper than I paid in the UK) – take a look at the local papers for a huge amount of suppliers, many of whom promise to deal with you in English.

140

You may also, eventually, need to get an MOT (**ITV**) on your vehicle. Again, this is different from the UK. The first ITV is due on your vehicle's **4th** birthday, and every **2nd** year thereafter up until it's **10th** birthday. After that, it's an ITV every year. You can take your car to your local ITV station yourself (you must make a prior appointment – easiest way is to do it online at http://circuitv.com/) or pay one of the numerous garages who advertise the service at around €35 in addition to the ITV fee (around €40) to pick your car up, get it tested and bring it back for you. I've done both, and I would definitely recommend getting somebody to do it for you; I managed to confuse the Spanish terms for "windscreen wipers" and "brakes", much to the amusement of the ITV Tester.

If you do want to do it yourself, take all the documents you got with the car, plus your insurance certificate, to your local ITV centre. Hand everything over – together with your fee – at the front desk. They will check everything, and then send you to queue at the actual technical area. One queue for cars and bikes, one for commercial vehicles. When it's your turn, drive over the inspection pit and follow your testers instructions with regard to braking, revving the engine, sounding the horn, turning on the windscreen wipers, etc. Or not, in my case! Assuming all is OK, you get your ITV certificate immediately. If you fail, you have to get the problem areas put right and then go for a re-test – your ITV station will give you the timescale for a free re-test.

Seems relatively simple so far? The fun starts if you really want to import a UK vehicle permanently into Spain. Legally, if you are a Spanish resident, and want to import a UK registered car, you have a period of **6 months** to re-register it, at which time you will get a Spanish number plate for the car. Again, many, many people do not bother to do this - within a 100m of our villa I can count at least 5 un-registered EU vehicles. If you are confident that you can get away with it, fine, but be warned – Tráfico are clamping down on illegal cars, and they will fine you if they notice your car has not been re-registered in the correct timescale.

The problem is not the procedure (as usual, you can do it yourself if you want to, although a **lot** of paperwork is involved); virtually everybody pays either an Abogado or a professional company to do it for them, but the cost.

To start with, all vehicles requiring re-registration must have a safety test (TARJETA DE INSPECCIÓN TÉCNICA) – this is applicable to both brand new and second hand vehicles.

If you are importing a **new** vehicle, then 21% IVA (vat) is payable. Yes, I know. You´ve already paid vat when you bought it in the UK. Hard lines, you have to pay again, against the Spanish book price.

Second hand vehicles (owned for more than 6 months by you, prior to you becoming resident in Spain) do not attract import duty, providing you paid the relevant VAT in the UK.

In addition to IVA (if applicable) you also have to pay a registration tax (*Impuesto Especial Sobre Determinados Medios de Transporte)*. This tax is based on the vehicle's market value and CO_2 emissions.

The paperwork you need is:

- Application Form (available from your local Tráfico or your agent will obtain it for you)

- ID (Residencia, passport)

- Proof of address (Escritura, lease agreement, Padron)

- Receipt for payment of car tax (available from your Ayuntamiento)

- Receipt for payment of registration tax

- Registration document

- Proof of IVA (VAT) payment

- Registration Fee

- Tarjeta de Inspeccion Tecnica

- Receipt for purchase of vehicle

- Certificate of Conformity (*Certificado de Conformidad*) from the vehicle manufacturer. There are 2 types; you need the EC Certificate, which is valid throughout the EU.

For each item, you need to present the original and a photocopy. A minor point amidst the plethora of documentation, but still needed – you must ensure that your car headlights are adjusted to Spanish standards.

Even if you are using an agent, you will have to pass on the relevant paperwork to him, but the agent will be able to advise what can and cannot be used, and will also complete the relevant forms and deal with Tráfico for you. Once you are successfully re-registered, your car will get a lovely new Spanish plate, and your likelihood of being stopped by Tráfico drops dramatically.

Moving swiftly on; what is the situation if you want to buy a *second-hand vehicle, from a private buyer?* And the answer is …. Yet more paperwork, I´m afraid.

You guessed it, you can "do it yourself" or employ an agent to do the transfer for you. Unusually, the agent in this case is normally a garage, and usually one that sells second hand cars themselves. Look in the local papers under "Services" for **somebody** who will do this for you. If you do use an agent, it´s normal for you and the seller to go along together to him to make the transfer. And a word of warning, whether you deal directly with Tráfico yourself, or use an agent, the tax will be calculated on the book value of the car in question, **not** what you paid for it. The relevant form is available from Traffico if you want to DIY.

You will also need:

- The Registration document (*permiso de circulación*)

- Technical sheet (*Ficha Tecnica*)

- The receipt for the road tax (*impuesto sobre la circulacion de vehiculos*)

- If you are doing it yourself, a receipt for the payment of transfer tax (8%) (normally paid by the seller, unless you agree otherwise). If you use an agent, they will do this for you and take the 8% at the time the transfer is made, passing it on to Tráfico.

You have 15 days to register the vehicle in your name. Although not a legal requirement, it´s a good idea to get all the details of your seller – obviously name and address, but also NIE and passport number, just in case of problems.

So, you have your vehicle. But what about your driving licence? If you have a UK "EU" style identity card driving licence, with your photograph on it, you **should** be able to use this to drive in Spain until its expiry date. I use the word "should" as there is so much controversy around this, it´s difficult to be sure about it.

I checked with the Guardia about this, and their advice was to get a Spanish licence. To do so, you have a 6 month grace period from the time you get your Residencia. On the other hand, there have been numerous articles published which insist that a UK "EU" driving licence should be valid throughout Europe, including Spain.

If you have the old style paper licence, then you definitely need to get a Spanish licence, as this type is not legal in Spain, if you are resident.

Assuming you have a UK "EU" licence, in order to be safe and happy driving in Spain, I suggest you either trade it in for a Spanish licence, or – if you really want to keep it – then go in for the Spanish "medical", for which you will get an additional certificate. The reason for this is that here have been several cases where holders of UK licenses who are resident, but who have not taken the medical, have been involved in car accidents and have found that their insurers have refused to pay up. Isolated incidents, admittedly, but better safe than sorry! Once your original UK licence expires, you must get a Spanish licence and at this point you will have to take the medical. This bit gets really complicated, and causes a huge amount of bother, but this is the advice I have been given by the Guardia:

-   If your current UK licence has not expired, and you apply for a Spanish licence, then your Spanish licence will be valid up to the expiry date on your UK licence. This is applicable to both paper and picture licenses. E.g., your UK licence expiry date is 2027, but you are exchanging it for a Spanish licence in 2015. In this case, your Spanish licence will not expire until 2027.

    In this case, **you do not have to take the "medical".**

- If you are obtaining a Spanish driving licence because your UK licence has expired, then your new licence will be valid up to the age of 65. **In this case, you do need to take the "medical".**

- If you are renewing a Spanish licence (they last for 5 years after the age of 65) **you will need to take the "medical".**

- **"The medical"** in question is a sight test, blood pressure reading and a test on a thematic perception machine, which measures your reaction to hazards on the road; i.e. it beeps frantically every time you run over the old lady who walks in front of your car on the screen. Don't worry about it – I have seen Spanish drivers in for the test who have more beeps than silences, and they still passed. In fact, if you get through without a beep, they make you do it again because they think the machine is faulty (honest!).

- The medical centers tend to be situated either in, or above, driving school centers. If it's very busy, they will ask you to make an appointment, otherwise, just wait for a slot.

To apply for your Spanish driving licence, you first need the relevant form obtainable from Tráfico in Alicante (**Ministerio Del Interior - Dirección General de Tráfico, C/** Josefa Valcárcel, 28027 Madrid Tel.: 902 88 70 60, websitehttp://www.dgt.es/es/). Complete this and return it with all the usual suspects (Padron, Residencia, NIE, passport + copies) and a copy of the back and front of your UK driving licence and paper counterpart (if it is a photo licence) or copy of your paper licence. You also need 2 photographs of the correct size – if you're using a photo booth, check, or tell your photographer that the photos are for a SPANISH driving licence. Again, any Abogado or accountant will assist you with this, for a standard fee. Tráfico will then contact DVLA in the UK, to confirm the details on your old licence. Allow at least 3 months for this process. I was deeply unfortunate, in that my application took a record 21 months! Not Trafico's doing, sad to say – they eventually contacted me in despair to ask if I would contact DVLA directly; Tráfico had applied for my information 3 times, and been given wrong, separate, dates each time.

On one occasion, DVLA cheerfully gave my licence expiry date as 1980 – the year my provisional licence expired! Still, I got there in the end.

Once all the information is received by Tráfico, they will issue you with a temporary licence. Keep this until your full licence arrives, which is generally a couple of weeks later. If you are driving, always carry your licence with you.

And a few miscellaneous bits about driving in Spain:

- Legally, you must carry with you a reflective vest (most people have 2, although you are supposed to have one for each of the driver and passengers); a spare set of headlight bulbs and a reflective warning triangle.

- If you are driving, you must have a valid driving licence with you, together with an ITV if applicable.

- Spanish driving licenses start with 12 points **on them.** If you commit an offence which incurs points, these are **deducted.**

- If you go through a tunnel, or substantial bridge, you **must** switch on dipped headlights.

- If you do not stop at a "stop" sign, no matter how well your view, you are liable to be fined and have points taken off your licence.

- If you fail to buy a ticket in areas where they are mandatory (look for the machine; either yellow or blue lines at the curb, or check to see if other drivers have tickets displayed) you will get a fine; you can put the money for this, together with your ticket, in the bottom of the machine that issues your ticket, or pay at any Post Office (Correos).

- If you have the misfortune to be towed away, check on the road where your car was – there may well be a plastic bag screwed up on the floor with your fine details in it. If this happens, go to the nearest Policia Local to pay, and get your car back.

- If you do get a fine, pay it as soon as possible. If you pay within 30 days, the amount owing is usually halved. After 3 months beyond the due date, it starts to increase.

- If you are parking in town, check carefully for signs that say "Mes Impar" (*odd month)* or "Mes Par" (*even month).* This means you can park on one side of the road on odd months, and the other on even months. If you can´t remember which is which, don´t park on the side which has no other cars!

- If you are traveling with a dog in your car, it has to be secured (either behind a dog guard, or harnessed to a fixed point). If it isn´t you can get a spot fine.

- Drinking and driving – don´t! Tráfico are very tough on drink driving, and the limit is low.

- If you are unfortunate to be in an accident, or witness an accident, stay put until the Guardia arrive. Failure to report and accident, or leaving the scene of an accident before the Guardia are there, is a fineable offence.

- Don´t drive in backless shoes or sandals. It´s an offence, and could lead to a fine if you are stopped by the Guardia for any reason.

- And finally, don´t think because you are driving a hire car you are exempt. Spain now has communication links with France and the UK, if you commit a traffic offence in Spain, then it will follow you to the UK!

Chapter 11

Pets in Spain

Of course you want to bring Rufus and Molly with you. They´re part of the family, of course they have to come with you to enjoy a new life in the sun. And – just for once – importing cats and dogs in to Spain is relatively straightforward. You do, of course, need to meet the relevant legislation but in this instance your local vet will do it all for you.

Once you have a date set for your move, talk to your vet. Cats and dogs both have to have a current "Pet Passport" which certifies that all their inoculations are up to date at the time of moving. Both cats and dogs have to be micro-chipped, and both have to have current rabies inoculations. The timescale seems to change quite regularly, so talk to your very well in advance of the move to ensure they are fully up-to-date. You will normally find that your vet wants to inspect your pet(s) shortly before they travel, to make sure that they are fit and well. The really good news is that you no longer have to put them into quarantine.

You can either import your pets yourself; most ferries now have "pet friendly" cabins, so you don't have to be parted from them for the journey. If you intend to fly across, I'm afraid they will have to go in the hold. The only exception to this is for very small dogs, where some (but far from all) airlines will let you keep them in the cabin, as long as they are fully secure in a bag or box that you can keep beneath your feet. Or, you can pay one of the many companies who will collect them from your home and deliver them to your new address in Spain. Whichever option you go for, you **must** have a valid pet passport for each pet.

Vets in Spain are quite a bit cheaper than in England, and are excellent. Most don't even need an appointment – just walk in and wait your turn. Once your pet is here, it's a legal requirement for dogs to have an annual rabies inoculation. Some "dangerous" breeds also require you to have insurance – check with your vet if your dog falls into this category.

In theory, all dogs over a certain size (apologies for being vague – this varies from area to area and from time to time) should be muzzled when you take them out. And all dogs should be kept on a lead. In practice, neither of these rarely happens! You will, however, be liable to incur a fine if your dog messes in a public place, and you don´t pick it up. Again, one of those laws that is often flouted, I´m afraid.

There are 2 potential hazards that you should be aware of; **leishmaniosis** for dogs, and **processional caterpillars** for both dogs and cats (and children).

Leishmaniosis (also known as "heart worm") is a potentially life-threatening disease for dogs. It´s transmitted by the bite of the sand fly. Once bitten, the fly lays it´s eggs in your dog, and these migrate to his heart, where they hatch as tiny worms. It´s an awful disease and dogs that are not killed by it have to take medication for life. It can be avoided, very easily, by either buying your dogs special collars (which also guard against ticks – not deadly, but a damn nuisance) which give 95% protection against leishmaniosis, and can be bought at all vets and most chemists. You will need 2 per year, although many people don't bother with them in the winter, when the sand flies are scarce. Cost varies with the size of dog, from around €20 to €40.

Very recently, you have also been able to get your dog inoculated against leishmaniosis. It costs around €100 for the initial procedure, which includes a blood test to ensure the disease is not present, and then a further 3 injections at weekly intervals. After that, you need a booster once every year (about €35 annually). This is 100% effective.

The disease is prevalent in marshy areas, or at the seaside, so if you live entirely in a town, it's less likely that you need to worry.

You may have sniggered at the second deadly hazard; processional caterpillars. Everybody always thinks you're joking – until they see them! These caterpillars start life on new growth on pine trees. You first see them in late autumn, when pine trees appear to be decorated with fuzzy, rather dirty "purses" of grey candyfloss. These "purses" are where the caterpillar eggs are incubating. They hatch in spring – depending on how warm and dry the winter has been – between February and early April. Everybody who has pets keeps an eye on the nests, and word quickly goes around when they are hatching (the caterpillars stay on the outside of the candyfloss for a few days before moving on). Often, residents clip off those nests they can reach, and burn them in metal buckets.

These caterpillars can be **deadly** to cats, dogs and small children. Even adults can have a very nasty reaction to them.

The reason they are called "processional" is obvious once they leave the nest. Only the first hatched caterpillar can see, and then only to differentiate between light and dark. As a result, the caterpillars leave the nest nose to tail, forming what looks exactly like a brownish rope, up to about a metre in length. If you come across them **do not touch them. Don´t let your dog or cat sniff them.** The caterpillars are covered in very loose hairs which are released at the slightest touch. These hairs are a gross irritant to the nasal passages, and inflame the skin. If your pet has got near enough to sniff, get water into their mouths as soon as possible (in the case of a dog, shove the hosepipe in his mouth, and keep it there for at least a minute) and then get them to the vet, urgently. Symptoms include frantic scratching at the muzzle and lips, obvious discomfort generally, and foaming (quite literally, foam dripping on the floor) at the mouth.

Our dog managed to find some caterpillars last year, when I was stupid enough to let him off his lead in the campo. It took me 5 minutes to get him home, by which time he was heaving for breath, foaming at the mouth and trying to wipe his muzzle on the pavement to get some relief. 10 minutes later, we were at the vet and he said another few minutes and we would have lost our dog. It's quite common for afflicted dogs to have to have part of their jaws removed, so bad is the reaction. I should add that I put my hand in our dog's mouth, in an attempt to wipe away any hairs that remained. An hour later, my thumb was twice it's normal size and shiny purple – that from second hand hairs! I was on anti-biotics for a week.

As with sand fly, you are far more at risk on urbanizations or in the country than in towns, but these caterpillars do appear anywhere there are pine trees. If you see the hatched caterpillars, if you possibly can, spray them with hair lacquer (stops the hairs flying out) and set fire to them. Yes, I know. Until we moved over, I would have shuddered and said it was cruel, as well. Having seen the damage they can do, I now keep a can of hair lacquer in the house (and I don´t even use the stuff on my hair!).

And finally …. Ginger or white cats. Cats love the heat. Our 2 gingers sprawl in it, contentedly, for hours, The problem is, ginger or white cats have very little pigment in their skin, and it´s very easy for them to get sunburned, or even – with constant exposure – skin cancer, particularly on their ears and noses. The answer? Buy a very high factor sun cream (factor 50 is excellent) or a total sun block, and sneak up on them to put it on the tips of their ears and their nose. They'll cause no end of a fuss the first few times, but they do get used to it (particularly if a treat is involved) and it gets easier after a while.

And I should mention that you are likely to find that if your pet needs medication (other than an injection) your vet will give you a prescription, which you can take to any chemist (Pharmacia) to get made up!

Chapter 12

Planning Permission

Sorry, back to the paperchase again!

Unlike the UK, you need planning permission in Spain for **anything** that is a permanent change to your structure. There are no exemptions! When I say "anything", I mean you need planning permission for things like:

- Low boundary walls, constructed of stone or breeze blocks

- Crazy paving, laid on existing concrete paths

- Tiles, laid on existing tiles

- Interior walls, constructed or taken down

- Internal or external doorways, opened up or blocked in

- Car ports, if they are anchored into concrete

- Small patios

The list is almost endless, and even worse, varies not just from town to town, but often from street to street, depending on whether it is new or old, or what the fascia is like. Bear in mind, it doesn't matter that the work is taking place within your existing footprint – for instance, converting an underbuild into an apartment. It still qualifies for planning permission.

However, it's not all bad news. Planning permission for minor works is generally easily obtainable. If you're doing the work yourself (and yes, it is not difficult to get planning permission for this) take a photograph of the location of the works. Draw a basic plan showing what you want to do, add a paragraph in Spanish explaining the extent of the work, and give an estimate of the cost. It's important to mark on the plan how close boundary walls – both neighbours and road –

are, as this is usually a major factor in obtaining permission. For instance, on our urbanization any "structure" has to be no nearer than 4m to a main road, and 3m to boundary fences/walls with neighbours´ gardens. The only exemption is for rooms which have doors but no windows and are to be used purely for storage ("trastero") when they can be as close as 2m to the neighbour´s boundary. Why? I have no idea, and I rather think the Ayuntamiento has forgotten why, as well!

In any event, take your plans and photograph down to the Ayuntamiento, to the department called "Urbano" or "Urbanismo". If everything is in order, they will give you a form to complete. You will get 2 copies of this, both stamped. Take both to whichever bank your Ayuntamiento instructs you to use, and hand over the planning fee (for small works, normally only a few euros) plus both copies. The bank will stamp one copy as paid, and return it to you. Take this back to the Ayuntamiento, who will take it off you. Anytime between a couple of days and a couple of weeks later, you will receive, in the post, a document headed "Licencia para Obras Minor" which is your planning permission. You generally have around 3 months from the date on the permission to complete the work.

If you are using a Contractor, he will get the planning permission for you, if you insist! It seems to be par for the course with Spanish builders that the opening gambit is always "Oh, you don´t need planning permission for this!" but if you insist that you do, they will shrug and get it for you. A word of advice – don´t let work commence until you have that piece of paper in your hand. Ayuntamientos are getting very keen on ensuring that planning permissions are in place, and it is increasingly common for them to send Planning Officers wandering around urbanizations, simply keeping an eye on any building work that is in progress. If they find that licenses have not been issued, they will stop work until all the paperwork is in order, and you may well get a fine on top of planning permission fees. If the work in question is illegal, they also have the power to demand that it is demolished. Also worth bearing in mind is that when you come to sell your property, your buyer's Abogado will want to see planning permissions for all work that has been done, and it´s not an easy process to get retrospective permissions. If it´s illegal, you will simply not be able to get the permission.

Major building work is more complicated. Firstly, for any major construction work (for instance, extensions) that qualify as "Obras Major" you must have an architect. **You will not get planning permission without one, and the architect must be registered with the Spanish College of Architects.** The architect will be expected to draw up a specification for the works, together with detailed drawings, and these must be presented to the Ayuntamiento, and permission given to proceed, before any work is undertaken. Many Ayuntamientos seem to be deeply suspicious of non-Spanish architects; when we had a large extension added to our villa some years ago, our absolutely excellent and superlatively qualified architect was Argentinean, which led to us getting a suspicious telephone call from our Ayuntamiento, demanding to know if his qualifications were recognized in Spain. We actually had to ask the poor man to take his certificates down to the Ayuntamiento, for their Architect to inspect, before we could proceed. All drawings will also have to be certified as correct by the College of Architects, and – of

167

course – the Ayuntamiento will also have to be satisfied that everything meets the relevant planning regulations. Once either you, or your architect, appoint a Contractor, the Contractor will then have to take the drawings and specification to the Ayuntamiento to get final building consent, both for the project and for him to do the work. Then, and only then, will you be issued with a "Licencia para Obras Mejor." Our Contractor tried to convince us we didn´t need an architect, which is really only par for the course. If yours does the same, don´t believe him!

Your architect will visit site at strategic intervals, to ensure the work is carried out correctly. You are also likely to find that the Ayuntamiento will also visit, to check, at intervals. Both your architect and Contractor will expect stage payments, based on either time or milestones in the project. Do not pay your Contractor anything upfront that exceeds a reasonable amount to buy materials. Whatever you do, never, ever pay him the full amount, or anything like it, upfront. It´s not a matter of dishonesty (or at least, generally not) it´s just that if work is plentiful, he is quite likely to pocket your money and then go and do a few smaller jobs he has had waiting. In the meantime, you wait, and wait, and wait…

Your architect will agree he is happy with the work on completion, and at this stage you will have a visit from the Ayuntamiento to sign it off as well. Once complete, you should inform your Abogado and have the new work added to your Escritura.

Please, remember that your Contractor cannot get planning permission without an architect. What he can get is permission to allow him to carry out the work. This **is not** the full planning permission, but many people have been duped into believing that they do have full planning permission when all they have is permission for the Contractor to undertake the work. In practice, the distinction is simple – if you have your "Licencia para Obras Major", specifying all the work you want to undertake, and signed, sealed, stamped and delivered by your Ayuntamiento, you're fine. Without it – do not proceed!

To give you an indication of costs, our Ayuntamiento charge €65 for each square metre of build we wanted to construct. Not cheap, but at least we could sleep easy in our new bedroom!

Chapter 13

Living in Spain!

At long last, the good bits!

And they certainly are. I apologise if the preceding chapters appear to have been all doom and gloom. You have to remember, most of it is a "one off" exercise (for instance, getting your paperwork sorted and accessing the Health Service) or only happens at intervals of years (buying a car, income tax, etc) and once you get into the habit of it, it's very little hassle. The problems start when you don't expect things, or nasties pop up that you have no idea how to deal with. But – I hope – the information you have already acquired reading this has helped to ensure that you are not taken by surprise.

Trust me; living on the Costa Blanca is wonderful. We have one of the best climates in the world; the culture is fabulous; the people delightful; the food and drink an absolute joy. And you can live very well, for very little. But you do have to change your shopping habits, and the way you eat. Also, come to think of it, even the time you eat!

We often find friends who have holiday homes here, or who come over to stay in rented villas, insist that the cost of shopping is as dear, or even more expensive, than it is in the UK. I explain to them that they have to learn to eat and shop Spanish style. By this, I do **not** mean that you have to exist on a diet of paella and olive oil. Far from it! In fact, the Spanish rarely actually eat paella in the evening – they say the rice "sits" too heavily on the stomach; paella is a lunch dish, not evening.

When I say "change the way you eat", I mean you need to forget the ready meals you had to buy when you were working, because you had no time to cook, and not time to enjoy your meals. Eating is a major part of Spanish life, at every time of the day, and the key to eating in Spain is simple – enjoy! Forget the plastic burgers, and cereal-filled sausages. Don´t bother with pastry-heavy Cornish (so called, a *real* Cornish pasty is a thing of great beauty) pasties and stodgy steak pies, where you´re looking for the filling. And don´t even think of stocking your freezer with ready battered fish and oven chips. The key to eating good food, and very cheap good food, in Spain is twofold; use Spanish shops, markets and supermarkets, and eat seasonally.

Spain imports very little food. You will find the odd bunch of bananas from the Canaries, and often – yum! – Brilliant quality Argentinean beef (try Argentinean strip beef for the BBQ; around €6 a kilo even as I write, and wonderful). Other than that, if food is out of season, the only places you will be able to buy it are English supermarkets, where it has been weeks in transit so has lost most of its taste, and is also very expensive. So you get back into the habit of eating food when it is in season, which also means it is at its best. And unlike the UK, as the season progresses and fruit, vegetables and salad items become more plentiful, the price goes way down. At the moment (early July), sprouts, cabbage of all varieties, cherries, asparagus, pears, early oranges and satsumas have all gone out of season, and will not be back on the shelves until next spring. But in their place I have been buying plums, apricots, the first grapes, avocados, peaches and papaguays ("doughnut peaches"), corn on the cob, masses of different tomatoes and lettuces, courgettes, aubergines.... All fresh. All cheap. All actually tasting of something – even the lettuce!

All Spanish supermarkets are excellent. And in this I include the discounters – Aldi and Lidl – which follow the Spanish trend of only selling food in season, and at incredibly good prices. Mercadona is a Valencian based supermarket, which has hardly any English brands (apart from the odd tin of Heinz baked beans) but sells excellent local produce at great prices. A large sliced loaf in the English supermarket – barely fit for toast – would cost me €2.50. In Mercadona, I buy an 800grm "pan rustica" (a freshly hand baked crusty loaf, still warm and smelling and tasting delicious) for €1! A large sliced brown loaf (28 slices) again costs €1. A large French stick? Sorry, they will not sell me a single one, but a bag of 4 will cost me €1.20. Mercadona´s fish counter is legendary – everything with gills known to man, and all fresh and waiting to be prepared by the chicas behind the counter any which way you want them, at no extra cost. So good, we frequently see fascinated holidaymakers actually taking photographs of the display!

Fish, of course, is wonderful generally. Bass, merluza (hake), tuna, salmon, cod – all are nearly always available, and much cheaper than in the UK. Fresher, too! Giant prawns – frozen or fresh – are an everyday treat (although make sure they are labeled "cocina", which means they are ready cooked. If it says "cruda" they are raw.). Meat is also good, and relatively cheap. Pork and chicken in every shape and form are fabulous; in our town we are lucky enough to have a butcher who sells nothing but all things chicken. She´s always busy, but well worth waiting for. A kilo of fresh chicken breast? €4.50. A dozen large, fresh eggs? €1.19. (Or last week, €1. She had a glut, she explained.). In the carnisseria (general butcher); a kilo of calves liver? €4. A whole shoulder of fresh Spanish lamb (a completely different cut to English shoulder, much longer and feeds 4 greedy people) around €7 – €8, depending on the season. And the markets! Oh, don´t get me started on the markets! Every vegetable and salad stuff you can name (and quite a few that you wonder about), all fresh. All cheap. Want the tops cut off your leeks? No problem. Outside leaves cut off your cauliflower? Of course. How about a taste of these grapefruits, before you buy? And don´t go for those white mushrooms, these brown ones are much better....

Alcohol, too, is still cheap. At Christmas I noticed Lidl in England were advertising a "bargain" Rioja for just under £6. I got the same bottle (I lie – I actually bought a dozen bottles) in our local Lidl for €1.99 each. Even the English cheeseboard was cheaper in our Lidl than it was in England! You can buy an excellent red wine any day of the week for around €1. Spirits, also, are cheaper than England.

You will also probably find that you are eating at different times to what you were used to in England. In summer, it´s simply too hot to eat a great deal in the daytime; we tend to follow sensible Spanish habits. Breakfast is a cup of coffee whilst it´s still cool enough to enjoy sitting outside. Later – around 10.00 – it´s time for *almuerzas*– a treat, especially if you are out and near a café. You'll see "almuerzas" advertised at every café. Basically, because the Spanish tend to go to bed very late, they don´t have time for breakfast, so stop around 10.00 for a mid-morning snack – almuerzas. These are normally something like a tostada (half a toasted French stick, either eaten plain with a drizzle of oil, or spread with seasoned, pulped tomatoes and oil) or a croissant, all normally accompanied by coffee, and more often than not a small brandy. Don´t be put off if you find the café is full of drivers of vans and lorries – when you get inside, you normally find beautifully laid tables in a spotless room, and excellent prices and service.

Lunch isn´t eaten before around 2.00, and is a light meal as it´s often too hot to bother. Dinner never gets to the table in summer before 9.00 in summer; most restaurants don´t start serving before 7:30 in the evening, and they expect you to take at least a couple of hours enjoying your meal.

And speaking of eating out, even on a tiny budget, you are spoilt for choice. The Costa Blanca has restaurants serving the full quota of international food – Thai, Chinese, Japanese, American (even plenty of MacDonald's, if you really must), English, French, Italian, Spanish – you name it, you can probably find it. If you want to splash out, there are Michelin starred restaurants (even one in the village of Els Poblets that has had a makeover by Gordon Ramsey) where you can spend €100 per head on a lavish tasting menu. If you can´t run to that, try the "Menu del Dia". Most restaurants have these, and **please** don´t ignore them because they are often ridiculously cheap. They are not only cheap, they are virtually always delicious, and amazing value for money.

The Menu del Dia originated with General Franco, who declared that every Spaniard would have the chance to have at least one good meal per day. Probably the only good thing he did. Now, the Del Dia is always available at lunchtime, and often in the evening (but worth checking it's both). Prices range from around €8.50 (generally in more out of the way villages) to about €12 (I would faint if asked to pay any more than this, but there is a former Michelin starred restaurant quite close to us that charges €35 for its Del Dia. When we win the Lotteria we will go, but not before.) For your money, you can expect to get 3 courses – with a choice at each – bread and alioli, and a drink or half bottle of wine per person.

Even better value, and well worth searching for, is "Piscina Bars". "Piscina" means swimming pool, and these bar/restaurants are situated next to the municipal swimming pool. The pool itself is free to use, and normally has sun beds and showers – it's a perk for rate payers, but no reason why you shouldn't take a dip, if you want to cool off. You'll normally find them in villages and small towns, and please don´t go "ugh" at the thought of eating at the municipal pool. The Piscina Bar will be sited adjacent to the pool, and often in a lovely setting in either grassed areas or an esplanade. The reason they are cheap is that whoever has the franchise for the restaurant also has to keep the pool in good order, and so the restaurant is subsidized by the local council. If they don´t have a menu Del Dia on offer at a good price, then they are one of the few which are not subsidized. They are wonderful places to watch the world walk by, as – especially at week-ends – they are usually crowded with Spaniards. Our local Piscina Bar charges €8.50, and for that you get salad, tapas, main course (always a choice of lamb, pork, chicken, steak or 3 varieties of fish) with vegetables and proper chips, pudding, half a bottle of wine, bread and alioli and coffee. And the portions are not small! And if you ask for a brandy or gin and tonic, they keep pouring until you say "when".... And on Saturdays, we have a Spanish trio, belting out everything from golden oldies to jazz and rock. And once a month in summer, a free outdoor cinema screen arrives. As good as it gets? You betcha!

If you fancy a Chinese, you really cannot go wrong in visiting one of the many "Woks". These are serve yourself buffets, with a huge range of food sushi, salads, rice dishes, grilled meats and fish and shell food (I even know several that serve oysters and lobster, in season, yum!) and, of course, the actual wok element where you select your food and sauce, and it is cooked for you, while you wait. Average cost? Around €10 for as much as you can eat. Occasionally, wine, beer and soft drinks are thrown in, in which case expect to pay about €13 for as much as you can eat and drink.

The only real problem with eating in Spain is trying to diet; I haven´t managed it, but I suppose if you put your mind to it, it might be worth a try.

There are times, of course, when only an English supermarket will do. When you are about to run out of Bisto, or want some Schweppes lemonade, or would die for a lump of vintage cheddar. But there is no way I would do my main shopping there! To give you an indication of the cost of living in the Costa Blanca North, the following is a rough guide to my normal expenses. There are 2 of us, plus 4 cats and a greedy Labrador; it´s a standing joke in our house that the animals´ food takes up more of the shopping trolley than our food.

- Weekly food shop: around €80

- Diesel (per month): €50

- Electric (per 2 months): Varies by season, depending on how much we use the air conditioning. In June, July and August, the answer is a lot! Between €150 - €220. We are on the "Dia y Noche" tariff, where electricity is half price for 14 hours a day (11.00pm – 1.00pm in summer, 10.00pm to 12.00 noon in winter) and fractionally dearer for the remainder of the day. It´s well worth having; to change your tariff, visit your nearest Iberdrola offices (www.iberdrola.es for details) and take along your last electric bill, your passport and NIE number. Ask for "Energia Dia y Noche". (For full details, of this tariff, visit https://www.iberdrola.es/clientes/hogar/luz/mas-10kw/energia-dia-noche).

And whilst on the subject of electricity, what do you do if you find your supply has been cut off, or – worse case scenario – you meter has disappeared? If your meter has gone (very unlikely, I have only know it happen once, unfortunately to a friend of mine who has a holiday villa here, and this was due to a total breakdown in communications) ring Iberdrola immediately. The number to speak to somebody in English is **900 225 235.** If you appear to have no electricity, check your fuse box first. If this is OK, grab a neighbour and ask if their supply has gone as well. If everybody else is connected, and your fuse box is OK, it´s likely that Iberdrola have disconnected you, generally because a bill has not been paid. This doesn´t have to be recent – I have known a payment to be missed 6 months before, but it has still led to a supply being disconnected. Normally, if you owe Iberdrola money they will send you a reminder, but occasionally communications break down and as a result the supply is cut off. If you are disconnected, ring the English speaking number, and have your credit or debit card handy, together with your electricity account number and your NIE number. Once the outstanding amount is paid, you should be connected again very quickly. If there is a problem, insist you have either a young child or very old person in the house – this usually does the trick. And don't worry – it doesn't happen often. Best to check your bank statement regularly, on line if possible, to make sure payments have been made.

- Gas: We have bottled gas, which I use only for the hob. A bottle currently costs €17.50, and last me around 9 months.

- Oil: We have oil-fired central heating. And sorry, in winter (end November to February) we find we are grateful for it. The combi- boiler also gives us instant hot water, and a 1000l tank lasts around a year. Depending on the cost of oil, between €700 - €800 per year.

- Car insurance and tax: Insurance €220 fully comprehensive. Tax (based on emissions) €57.

- Telephone, VOIP, internet connection:
All with the same supplier; not the cheapest around, but probably the most reliable. Around €50 per month, as we get some free calls to Spain and Europe. Be warned, your internet speed is unlikely to be as fast as in the UK, I have 3mb, which is fine, but if you want more, you have to pay more.

- IBI (Council tax) €550 per year (for a 2 bedroom house on a 500sm plot), + €150 for "basura" (rubbish collections).

- Water – generally metered, and varies widely from place to place. In the drier areas, you may have to buy "cubes" of drinking water. Ours is rarely more than €20 per month, and I pour lots on the garden year round.

- Satellite TV: Freeview is widely available, either by buying a box (about €80) and a dish (varies enormously by size – check out the local adverts) or paying around €5 per month. You can also get Sky, albeit illegally, although everyone does. Both buy a SKY box and card (again, see local adverts) or bring your own box and card over. If you get a card here, you will be charged an exorbitant "accommodation fee" of around €150 per year to convince SKY you are in the UK, in addition to a monthly fee. You can also pay to get SKY directly through your internet connection; again, see adverts for prices. This is generally cheaper, but the drawback is, if your internet goes down, so does your SKY...

Generally, white goods and furniture are more expensive here than in the UK. We do have Ikea, although only 2 branches on the Costa Blanca to date, and DFS in Alicante will deliver to the Costa Blanca South. Argos Spain will sell you a wide variety of goods, but only those small enough to be delivered by 1 man. Marks and

Spencers, John Lewis, Evans, Cotton Traders and Yours Clothing all deliver to Spain, at very reasonable rates. You can, of course, buy in the UK and have items shipped over.

And a word of warning; it´s impossible to do a "one stop shop" in Spain. Some large supermarkets (such as Carrefour) carry electric goods and domestic linen, etc. Some larger supermarkets carry a range of magazines and newspapers. All supermarkets sell alcohol. But by and large, if you want a newspaper or magazine, you have to go to a newsagent. No supermarkets sell cigarettes or tobacco – for these, you must go to a tobacconist. No shops, other than a chemist (*Pharmacia*, clearly recognizable by a large green cross outside) sell anything vaguely medical – even for a packet of paracetamols, or a tube of antiseptic ointment, you must visit a Pharmacia. And the one, weird, exception to the rule? You can´t buy stamps in the Correos (Post Office)! They will happily frank your letters and parcels for you, but they don´t stock stamps.

Also worth bearing in mind, other than supermarkets and some larger garden centers, most shops still close for 3 or 4 hours in the afternoon for a siesta (properly called *"medio dia"*). Generally, expect local shops to be closed from 1 to around 4 or 5. They then re-

186

open to at least 8 or 9 at night.

And you will frequently see vans parked at the side of the road, with a little stand outside. These guys sell oranges and lemons all year round, and other fruit when it is in season. The year starts with cherries in early June, moves on to asparagus, then peaches, melons, watermelons (*sandia)* and wild mushrooms (*ceps)*. They only ever have the one item for sale, but it´s well worth buying as it is always fresh, and relatively cheap. Only problem is that you have to buy large quantities; 2 kilos for cherries and peaches and whole fruits for melons and watermelons.

Moving on to markets. I love a good market, and here on the Costa Blanca, you are spoiled for choice. Markets are generally of 2 types; general, where you can buy anything from fruit and vegetables to clothes and shoes, and "Rastros" which may sell some food and clothes, but are really the equivalent of flea markets in the UK.

Both types are great fun, and you can pick up some great bargains.

And here they are (apologies if I have missed your local event)

General Markets

Monday

Denia – Next to Mercadona supermarket (HUGE market, go early to get a parking space)/Callosa d´Ensarria/Castellon/Peniscola/Sagunto

Tuesday

Altea (On the sea front) Elda/Jalon/Jijona/Sagunto/Xativa/La Cala de Finestrat

Wednesday

Teulada/Benidorm – Near the Pueblo Hotel in the Levante beach area. (Another gigantic market – very popular with tourists, hence quite a lot souvenir type stalls. Nice for a wander around, but do take care of your wallet and bag – a prime target for pickpockets)/Alcoi/Orba/Polop de la Marina

Thursday

Javea (The Old Town. Can be difficult to park, but a very good general market)/Villajoyosa/Villena/Vinaros/Alicante/

Pego/Lliria/Cocentaina/Cullera

Friday

Moraira (Carretera Moraira Calpe. Another huge market, plenty of parking and on the flat. Great fruit and vegetable stalls)/Torrevieja – New Torrevieja Urban Area/Alfaz del Pi/Oliva/Onil/Petrer/Teulada/Vergel

Saturday

Benissa/Alcoi/La Cala de Finestrat/Calpe (Avenida del Norte)/Alicante/Gandia (In the market area at the end of Passeig de les Germanies in the old area of the town)

RASTROS

Wednesday

Calpe – Avda. Pais Valencia

Friday

Denia – Torrecremada

Saturday

Jalon (Main Jalon Alcalali Road)/Pedregeur (Just off N332)/Alfaz del Pi (Also Sunday)/Benissa/Callosa d´Ensarria

Sunday

Aigues de Busot/Alicante (Plaza del Ayuntamiento (Town Hall Square))/Teulada (Just entering the town from the N332)/Villajoyosa (In the Old Town)/La Nucia (Calle Porvilla)/Benidorm (Partida de Sanz) Beniarbeig.

And when you get tired of shopping, and markets and eating … why then, there´s the fiestas! Every town and village has it´s own, but there are some – the major events – that happen everywhere, albeit with a local flavour.

The fiesta calendar starts on 5th January, with the celebration of The 3 Kings. Christmas is celebrated more in Spain these days, but the real festival is The 3 Kings. This is the day that the 3 Kings arrive, with a huge parade and sweeties thrown to the children. This is also the day that children, traditionally, get their Christmas presents. If you are in a town by the sea, the 3 Kings arrive by boat. Denia's 3 Kings is particularly impressive, with the parade generally including not only horses, but real camels! A jolly, family event, very good humoured.

February is St. Antony's Day, and the Blessing of the Animals. This is lovely. Most towns (and quite a lot of animal shelters) hold this event. A local priest deputises as St. Antony, and blesses just about every type of animal you might find as a farm animal or pet. I've seen children bringing cats, dogs, rabbits and even goldfish to be blessed, standing in line with beautifully decorated goats and sheep! As usual, there is quite a lot of eating involved afterwards.

This is followed by the week-end before Lent, which is Carnival in many places! Parades, events – generally, a fun time before the austerities of Lent. Beats Pancake Day, anytime.

March is generally the Fallas. This is a totally Spanish event, and great fun. Every town suddenly sprouts huge (and I mean huge – often 20 or 30 feet high), highly coloured "floats". These can make fun of local dignatries, or just follow a theme. They used to be made of papier mache, but these days are usually polystyrene. All the floats are judged, and the winners are set on fire, with the 1st place burning last. Generally, there's lots of food and drink involved, not to mention fireworks (fireworks set off during the day are called "macletas" and are all noise and no colour).

June brings bonfires – generally on beaches. Traditionally, families gather on the beach on the night of San Juan, light bonfires and – you guessed it – eat and drink a lot. Very touchingly, at midnight everybody walks into the sea, and makes a wish for the coming year.

July is "Festival of the Sacred Blood or our Lord Jesus Christ", generally noted for parades, fireworks, childrens events, dancing and "Bous a la Mar"; literally, "Bulls to the Sea." Many seaside towns erect mini bullrings, with lots of seating, and for a couple of days, twice a day, the local young men (and not so young, but definitely as stupid) tease the bulls into the sea, generally falling in themselves in the process. Quite often, the bulls manage to remain on dry land, whilst the idiots who are chasing them end up in the sea, but as far as I can tell, neither bulls nor partipants seem to worry about it greatly.

Depending on your location, June/July and sometimes August is Moors and Christians. If you´ve never seen a Moors and Christians, you don´t know what your missing! They are supposed to celebrate the victory of the Christians over the invading Moors, in the middle ages, and almost everywhere the Christians win. But the show is breathtaking. Mock castles are erected, battles are fought and parades (with costumes you will not believe) go on for hours. First the Christians parade/walk/dance by, and then the Moors have their turn. Even very small towns put on tremendous shows, with parades that go on for hours, and the whole event generally lasts for around 3 days with parades and fireworks. The best one I have seen is at Alcoi de Mura; this one is so famous and so spectacular, there is even a museum in Alcoi dedicated to the festival.

And although not strictly a "fiesta", 1st of November is a bank holiday in Spain. This is the "Dia del Morte" (Day of the Dead) when families congregate in the local cemetaries to honour their dead. It is very traditional, and very moving.

Apart from the national fiestas, every village and town has its own, additional events. For instance, in September, Denia holds the "Burial of the Sardine". This is quite sombre, with participants dressed in black with a tear painted on their cheeks. However, after a while the fireworks start, and the food and drink starts flowing, and miraculously everybody begins to have a really good, noisy time.

Many small villages have a wonderful event every few years, called a "Festeria". A queen of the Festeria is chosen (an event which nearly bankrupts her parents, as the day clothes, evening dresses, specially embroidered sashes, photographs, etc, can amount to an outlay of as much as €10,000) and every young person in the village of a certain age takes part. There are parades, pageants, feasts... this is also probably your only chance to actually get to see inside "ordinary" village houses, as the doors and windows are thrown open wide for the duration of the parades. Call me nosy if you like (and as I am, I will not be in the least offended) but I find it fascinating to peer into these lovely houses, which – in the Moorish tradition which says you should shun ostentation, and hide your wealth and belongings – are normally well and truly shuttered. The principle of the Festeria is that the young people are

194

symbolically "married" to the village, so even if they roam far afield, they will return. Now, isn't that lovely?

Enyoy! Take part – nobody will think it odd that a foreigner is celebrating with them. It's part – and a large part – of living in Spain.

Unfortunately, also a part of living in Spain is dying in Spain. Not a subject anybody wants to think about, but I feel I should at least touch on the protocol.

Worth remembering, when you die in Spain, in common with most hot countries, you are buried or cremated quickly – generally within 48 hours. If you want to give your loved ones time to come over to attend the funeral service, then you will have to pay extra for each day the deceased is kept in the mortuary. If you want the body to be repartriated to the UK, reach for your credit card, it isn't cheap.

Generally, there are 2 ways to be "buried" in Spain. As with the UK, you can choose to be cremated. If you want to be buried, there are a few English style cemataries about, but few and far between. Generally, people are "buried" in "Cemetarias" which are actually ossuaries – all the burial plots are above ground, in tiers in what are called "streets". They are actually like cities, filled with the dead. Each "grave" has a permanent stone or marble or wood marker, closing off the entrance, and generally giving a few details about the deceased. It may sound gruesome, but it isn't. These Cemetarias are quiet, beautifully kept and very, very tranquil. Relatives come to sit with their loved ones, and have a chat. I have made it clear that when I go, I want to move to our local Cemetaria, thank you! Put my Kindle in with me, and I'll be fine for all eternity.

As in the UK, funerals can be expensive in Spain, and normally the Funeral Director wants paying immediately, before, rather than after, the funeral.

There are a number of companies (see the local press for details) who will, for either a one-off fee, or a series of payments at intervals, take care of all your funeral arrangements for you. These plans are inflation proofed, and also have the advantage that all the administration is taken care of for you, at the time you need problems the least. Literally, one 'phone call to alert the company and the funeral arrangments etc are all made. The best plans can also be transferred to the UK, if you move back, and can –

depending on the company involved – be valid in other EU countries such as Portugal and Cyprus. Check what is offered from a couple of companies before buying.

A couple of companies actually knock on your door and try to sell you a plan. As always, the choice is yours, but be aware that there is more than one company out there.

Chapter 15

Pensionistas´ Perks!

I´m delighted to say, there are quite a few of these in Spain.

On a local level, as a Pensionista, you will be entitled to discounts to enter the municipal indoor pool and gym – in practice, this means it will cost you about €1 to swim for as long as you want, and another euro to use the gym and sauna. You can also join the local "Pensionista" club, where drinks and food are discounted, and cheap "outings" arranged. Many Pensionistas clubs also have numerous "events clubs" where you can learn to play bridge, learn Spanish, learn Spanish cookery, etc.

In both places, just show your passport and padron. Some (although not all) Ayuntamiento´s give a discount on IBI charges to pensioners – check out the website, or ask at the front desk.

You also get more favourable income tax allowances – an extra €1000 approx. each when you reach 65, and a further €1000 at 70.

Whilst there's no such thing as a bus pass per se on the Costa Blanca (just as well, bus services tend to less frequent than they are in the UK), if you live in Alicante, or near enough to take advantage of it, you can get a pensioner's travel card for the city trams and buses which reduces the cost of bus/tram travel in the city from €1.25 to 75 cents within the city limits. You also qualify for good discounts if you are travelling on public transport to El Campello or Benidorm. You also qualify for heavily discounted rail travel. A "RENFE" (Spanish Train Service) travel card for pensioners (in this case, over 55's) costs an amazing €5, and gets you up to 40% discount on rail travel throughout Spain. (25% at week-ends). The trains are generally clean and comfortable, and often fast – a superb way of seeing the country. You can obtain your railcard (by showing your passport and giving your NIE number) at all main train stations.

And finally, what about a cheap holiday – or 2, 3 or 4? Yes, the Spanish Governemtn really does offer cheap holidays to pensioners, no matter what their nationality, as long as they are resident in Spain. I know it sounds to good to be true, but it´s actually common sense – the holdiays are only offered out of season, so it fills hotels that would otherwise have been half empty. You can holdiay on the Spanish mainland, the Balearics, Canary Islands and even Portugal! All the offers are amazing value, and generally include travel, accommodateion and meals. To give you examples of holidays offered in 2012/2013:

8 days	Andalucía	198€ per person
8 days	Portugal	208€ per person
10 days	Canary Islands	379€ per person
15 days	Andalucía	358€ per person
5 days	Cultural tour	235€ per person

And the scheme generally uses 3* and 4* hotels!

You have to register, but just for once, it´s easy. Go
to   http://www.abacotaxes.com/subsidised-holidays-
spain-imserso for full details – registering doesn´t commit
you to antyhing.

And that, I believe, is that! Please don't let the apparent complexities of buying and living in the Costa Blanca put you off; don't forget, most things are either done only once a year (like income tax) or at wide intervals. Once you have your forms, and are registered on the health system, you are in calm water! It's simply because the systems are different to what we have become used to in the UK, and, of course, there is always the language problem. Take it one day at a time, and don't worry – there's always mañana….

We are living, breathing testament to the fact that living here is wonderful. We have literally never regretted the move for one minute of one hour of one day. The bureaucracy can be frustrating, but when I listen to friends who have decided to move back to the UK, I realise I would now find things even more difficult in the UK than I ever do here. Learn to relax; learn to enjoy life again here in the sun.

I have taken great care to ensure that all the information in this Guide is accurate and up to date. If you find anything confusing – or God forbid! – incorrect, please drop me an e-mail and let me know. Generally, if I can help with anything, I will be pleased to try.

I should add that everything is likely to change if the UK decides to leave the EU at some time after the referendum in 2017. If this happens, what the future holds for any of us ex pats, both here on the Costa Blanca and Europe-wide, will take a crystal ball to predict. I can only say that from our point of view, the changes would have to be earth shaking to persuade us to move back to the UK.

Bienvenidos a España!

Acknowledgements and Disclaimer

With grateful thanks to the following individuals and websites, in no particular order:

HM UK Foreign Office
HM British Embassy, Madrid
HM Revenue and Customs
Salud Valencia
HR Services (Moraira)
Francisco Javier Artés Vallet
Millie Munro Services
Abaco Taxes
Spain Made Easy
Think Spain!
Costa Blanca News
Anglo Info
HM Department of Work and Pensions, UK
Dirección General de Tráfico
Ministerio del interior, Madrid
Europa EU
Puma 22
Pego Ayuntamiento
DVLA UK
Expat Focus
INSS Spain
Repsol Spain
Iberdrola Spain
Spain Accountants
CDF Architecture

Please note that I am not professionally qualified to give legal, financial or taxation information in Spain. This Guide is intended as a fairly light-hearted introduction to retiring to the Costa Blanca, and as such is a compilation of my own experiences as an ex-pat living on the Costa Blanca, and information obtained from a wide variety of sources. The information contained in this Guide is intended for general guidance only. The application and impact of laws and regulations can vary widely from time to time and the application of them to you is based on your individual circumstances, of which I have no knowledge. Given the changing nature of laws, rules and regulations I cannot guarantee that there are no omissions or inaccuracies in information provided. Accordingly, the information in this Guide is provided on the understanding that the author is not engaged in rendering legal, accounting, tax, or other professional advice and services. As such, this Guide **must not** be used as a substitute for consultation with professional accounting, tax, legal or other competent advisers. Before making any decision or taking any action, you must consult the relevant professional.

While I have used my best endeavours to ensure that the information contained herein has been obtained from reliable sources, I am not responsible for any errors or omissions, or for the results obtained from the use of this information. All information in this site is provided "as is", with no guarantee of completeness, accuracy, timeliness or of the results obtained from the use of this information, and without warranty of any kind, express or implied. In no event will I be liable to you or anyone else for any decision made or action taken in reliance on the information in this Guide or for any consequential, special or similar damages howsoever these may arise.

Certain links in this site connect to other websites maintained by third parties over whom I have no control. Because of this, I make no representations as to the accuracy or any other aspect of information contained in other websites.

Printed in Great Britain
by Amazon.co.uk, Ltd.,
Marston Gate.